W9-BSL-303

Entry into Citizenship

Aliza Becker
with Mary Ann Siegel

CONTEMPORARY BOOKS

a division of NTC/CONTEMPORARY PUBLISHING GROUP
Lincolnwood. Illinois USA

Acknowledgments

The author and publisher would like to thank the following people for their help and contribution to *Entry into Citizenship*.

Reviewers

Peggy Dean
Adult Learning Resource Center
Des Plaines, IL

Rachel Porcelli
Hollywood, FL

Gail Weinstein, Ph.D
Professor, San Francisco State University
San Francisco, CA

Heide Spruck Wrigley
Senior Researcher for Language, Literacy, and Learning
Aguirre International
San Mateo, CA

ISBN: 0-8092-0642-0
Published by Contemporary Books,
a division of NTC/Contemporary Publishing Group, Inc.
© 2000 NTC/Contemporary Publishing Group, Inc.,
4255 West Touhy Avenue, Lincolnwood (Chicago), Illinois 60712-1975 U.S.A.

0 1 2 3 4 5 6 7 8 9 M&GUNN 12 11 10 9 8 7 6 5 4 3 2 1

Contents

Introduction

Entry into Citizenship is a citizenship preparation text for non-native English speakers. Using a highly visual, minimized language format, it can be used with students from beginning through low-intermediate English proficiency. It is designed to be adapted to the needs of multi-level classes. The text is intended to be used with the *Entry into Citizenship Teacher's Activity Guide.* The companion text provides direction and specific activity ideas to adapt the text to students with varying levels of English proficiency.

Units 1–4 present the N-400, taking students through the complicated form one step at a time. In addition to helping students with the form, many commonly asked questions are answered, such as "Should I tell the INS about my traffic tickets?" and "How should I act in the interview?" Units 5–12 cover the civics and history components of the test. Each chapter begins with a picture and comprehension questions that address the content of the chapter. A Warming Up activity then addresses interpersonal and cultural issues that students may encounter when taking the test or the interview. The content follows, focusing largely on the N-400 form in Part One, and the 100 questions in Part Two. Additional information is included to provide a context for the required content. In addition, some content has been added because of its relevance to becoming a new citizen. Voting, for example, is presented in greater detail than would be required by the test. Chapters conclude with dictation, practice activities, and a written test largely consisting of multiple-choice questions from the 100 questions.

At present, the content of the dictation and other aspects of the test vary from district to district and even among individual officers. When the test is standardized, it should minimize this variation. It is incumbent upon the instructor to find out the test content used in the local INS district and to prepare students accordingly. Naturalization is a fairly routine process for most applicants, however, for some it can result in serious problems. The immigration file is reopened when the application is received by INS. Those areas in which it is advisable to seek legal counsel are noted in the text and Teacher's Activity Guide.

Unit 1
BEGINNING THE PROCESS

Most immigrants and refugees complete these steps to become U.S. citizens. The process for people who were not born in the United States to become citizens is called *naturalization*.

Preview

Find these things in the pictures.

fingerprint   Form N-400   interview   photo   swearing-in ceremony   test

U.S. Department of Justice
Immigration and Naturalization Service

APPLICATION FOR NATURALIZATION

OMB #115-0009

Who was George Washington?

Starting Out

Most people go through these steps to become naturalized citizens. Do you know the order of the steps? If you do, number the boxes.

1

Warming Up

Understanding the Interview

You will have an interview with an INS officer. This interview is one step in the citizenship process.

What can you say when you don't understand?

There are many possibilities. Here are some.
Please repeat that.
Please repeat that more slowly.
Please say that in a different way. I'm not sure what you mean.
I'm sorry. I don't understand.

Now look at the picture and complete the conversation. Use the sentences above to help you.

INS Officer: Did you have any problem getting here?

You: _____

INS Officer: Raise your right hand.

You: _____

INS Officer: How do you spell your last name?

You: _____

INS Officer: Can I please see some identification?

You: _____

Practice with a Partner

Say your conversations.

Understanding the Interview

Following Directions

Read the conversation.

INS Officer: Please remain standing and raise your right hand. Do you swear to tell the truth and nothing but the truth, so help you God?

Tomas: Yes.

INS Officer: Have a seat. Can I see some identification?

Tomas: Yes. Here it is.

Practice with a Partner

Say the conversation.

The INS Officer may tell you to do these things. Match the sentences with the pictures. Write the number of the correct sentence in the box.

1. You can sit down.
2. Stand up.
3. Remain standing.

4. Can I see some identification?
5. Do you swear to tell the truth?
6. Please raise your right hand.

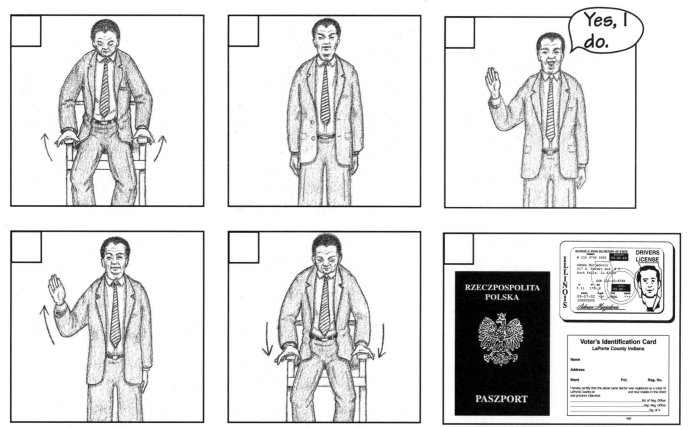

Requirements for U.S. Citizenship

A *requirement* is something you need or have to do. You must meet these requirements to become a U.S. citizen.

Check the box for each requirement you meet now.

Be age 18 or older.

Have no long absences from the United States.

Be a permanent resident of the United States for at least five years.
*There are exceptions. See page 11.

Pass a U.S. history and government test.

Pass an English test.

Have good moral character.

Be loyal to the United States.

Passing the Test

Telling the Truth

Who is telling the truth? Who is telling a lie?

Words to Know

arrest
truth
oath

An *oath* is a promise to tell the truth. At the INS interview, you take an oath to tell the truth.

Read this story.

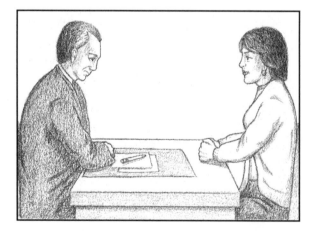

INS Officer: Have you ever been arrested?

Joana: No.

INS Officer: Are you sure?

Joana: Yes, I'm sure.

INS Officer: I can see in your criminal record that you were arrested for shoplifting last year. You are not telling the truth.

Joana: I'm sorry.

INS Officer: You cannot become a U.S. citizen now. You lied to the INS. You will have to wait 5 years, then apply again.

Practice with a Partner

What is an *oath*?
Why is it important to tell the INS officer the truth?

Understanding the Interview

Useful Language

The INS officer may ask you this question.

INS Officer: Why do you want to become a U.S. citizen?

You: Because I want to . . .

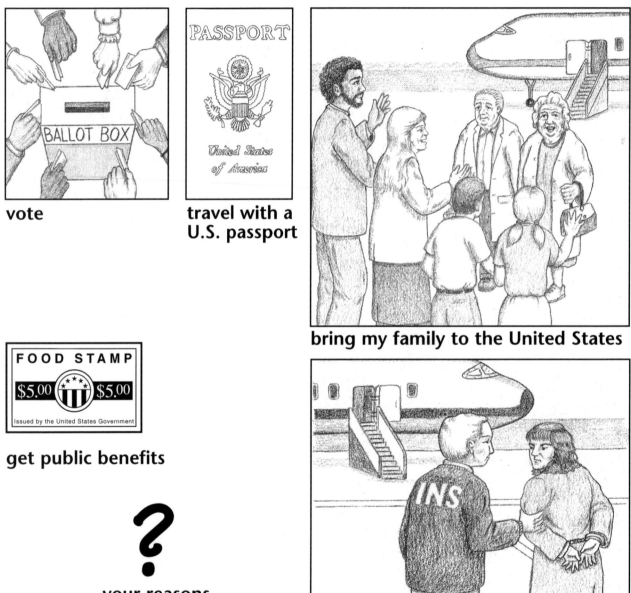

vote

travel with a U.S. passport

bring my family to the United States

get public benefits

your reasons

never be deported

Practice with a Partner

Why do you want to become a U.S. citizen?

Filling Out the N-400

Name Questions

Say the names of the letters of the alphabet. Spell your full name.

A   B   C   D   E   F   G   H   I   J   K   L   M

N   O   P   Q   R   S   T   U   V   W   X   Y   Z

Circle and spell on the permanent resident card:

Family (last) name

Given (first) name

Middle initial

permanent resident card

Note: permanent resident card = green card = alien registration card

Practice with a Partner

What is your given (first) name?
What is your family (last) name?
How do you spell your full name?
Do you have a middle initial? What is it?

Practice with a Partner

Fill in the chart.

What is your	Given (first) name?	Middle initial?	Family (last) name?
	Maria	L.	Perez
You			
Classmate			

Filling Out the N-400

Name Questions

Suey Lee Chen legally changed her name to Suey Lee Tsao when she got married. Her maiden name was Chen. Her married name is Tsao.

Suey Lee Chen

Ying and Suey Lee Tsao

What is your current name?

What is your name as it appears on your permanent resident card?

Rashid Mohammed uses another name at work. They call him Rich.

Have you ever used other names since becoming a permanent resident?

What name?

Practice with a Partner

What is your current legal name?
What is your name exactly as it appears on your permanent resident card?
Have you ever used other names since you became a permanent resident?

Filling Out the N-400

Changing Your Name

When you become a U.S. citizen, you can legally change your name if you take the oath in front of a judge. Some people choose a new name. Others do not.

Circle *yes* or *no*.

Do you want to change your name when you become a U.S. citizen?
    yes   no

Check your reasons.

Yes	No
I don't like my name. _____	I like my name. _____
My name is too long. _____	I am proud of my family name. _____
I want an American name. _____	I don't want a new name. _____
Americans won't understand my name. _____	Your own reason _____

Words to Know

abbreviations
initials

If you want to change your name, print the new name you would like to use. Do not use initials or abbreviations when printing your name.

Family Name (Last Name)

_____

Given Name (First Name)

_____

Full Middle Name

_____

Practice with a Partner

Do you want to legally change your name? Why?

Filling Out the N-400

Words to Know

basis
eligibility
lawful
qualify

Eligibility

The INS will ask you if you qualify to be a U.S. citizen.

Note: qualify = meet the requirements

Check the box for the requirement you meet. Check only one box.

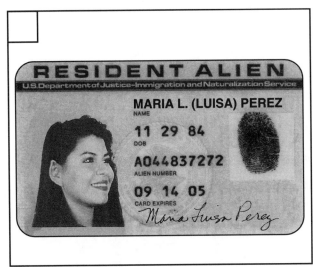

A. I have been a lawful permanent resident for at least 5 years.

B. I have been a lawful permanent resident for at least 3 years and have been married to a United States citizen for those three years.

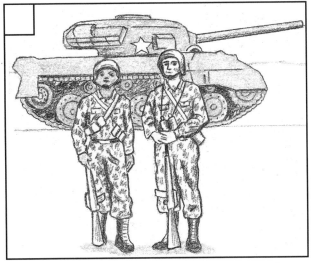

C. I am applying on the basis of qualifying military service.

D. Other (please explain) _____

_____

_____

Words to Know

permanent resident card
= alien registration
card = green card
alien card number = INS
"A" number

Alien Card Number

Fill in the blanks.

1	2	____	4	____
one	____	three	four	five

6	7	8	____	10
____	seven	eight	nine	____

RESIDENT ALIEN

U.S.Department of Justice-Immigration and Naturalization Service

MARIA L. (LUISA) PEREZ
NAME

11 29 84
DOB

A044837272
ALIEN NUMBER

09 14 05
CARD EXPIRES

Maria Luisa Perez

Read the alien card number.

You will need to write your "A" number in the top corner of each page of the N-400.

Write your INS "A" number here:

A ____ ____ ____ ____ ____ ____ ____ ____ ____

Practice with a Partner

What is your "A" number?

Dictation Practice

The citizenship test often has one or two dictation sentences. An INS officer reads a sentence aloud. Then you must write the sentence. This is practice for the dictation.

Read the words below aloud. Circle the first letter you hear in each word. Copy the word in parentheses that has the same first sound.

1. today   _____
                (test, flag)

2. sunny   _____
                (seat, red)

3. vote   _____
                (Washington, very)

4. American   _____
                (amendment, English)

5. permanent   _____
                (passport, test)

6. citizen   _____
                (seat, last)

Unit 1 Review

With a partner practice the interview and answer the questions.

INS: Stand up. Raise your right hand, please. Do you promise to tell the truth and nothing but the truth, so help you God?

You: I do.

INS: Take a seat, please.

You: Thank you.

INS: Can I see your passport, your green card, and another picture ID?

You: Here.

INS: Thank you. Do you understand the word *oath*? (page 5)

You: Yes, I do.

INS: What is an oath?

You: _____

_____

INS: Now we'll go over your application to see if there are any changes. What is your full name?

You: _____

INS: Have you used another name since you became a permanent resident?

You: _____

INS: The courts that perform swearing-in ceremonies also allow applicants to change their name when they become citizens. Would you like to legally change your name?

You: _____

Unit 2
TALKING ABOUT YOURSELF

Starting Out

- What is happening in this picture?

- How does the citizenship applicant feel?

Note: citizenship applicant = person who applied to become a citizen

Warming Up

Becoming a Citizen

How do you feel about becoming a U.S. citizen? Circle *yes* or *no*.

excited	yes	no
worried	yes	no
relaxed	yes	no
scared	yes	no

How do you relax when you are worried or scared?

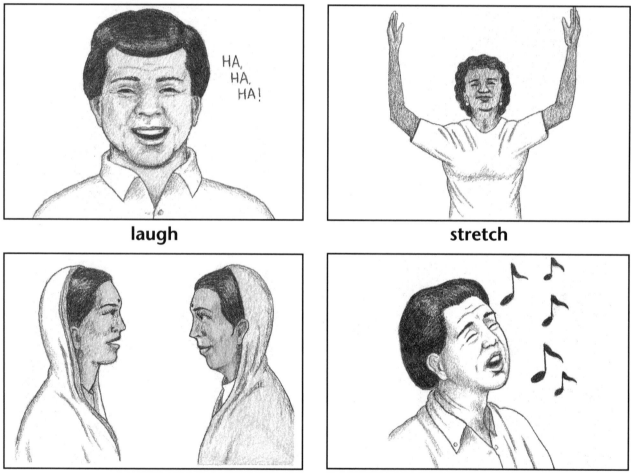

laugh

stretch

talk to someone

sing

Practice with a Partner

What do you do to relax?

Social Security Number

Read the social security number.

SOCIAL SECURITY

123-45-6789

THIS NUMBER HAS BEEN ESTABLISHED FOR

MARIA L. PEREZ

Maria Luisa Perez

SIGNATURE

Write your social security number.

_____

Practice with a Partner

What is your Social Security number?

Filling Out the N-400

Dates

You will need to write many dates on the N-400.

The year is usually divided into two numbers.
1776 = 17 + 76 = "Seventeen seventy-six"

When the number has a zero after the first number, we say "oh" before the number.
2002 = 20 + "o" + 2 = Twenty "oh" two.

In the United States, we read and write dates as month + day + year.
October 31, 1997   10/31/97

Practice

Circle the years as your teacher reads.

1777   1776   2002   2000

1991   1981   1990   1995

Draw a line to the correct date.

July 4, 1986   1/18/68

January 18, 1968   7/4/86

Date of Birth

What is your date of birth?

_____

month/day/year

Filling Out the N-400

Date You Became a Permanent Resident

The date you became a permanent resident is the date you received your permanent resident card.

1989–1995

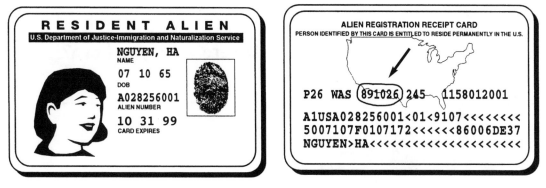

What date did she become a permanent resident?

_____

month/day/year

1996 or later

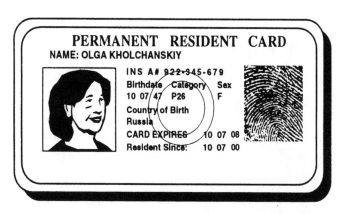

What date did she become a permanent resident?

_____

month/day/year

Practice

When did you become a permanent resident of the United States (permanent resident adjustment date)?

_____

month/day/year

How long have you been a permanent resident? _____

Filling Out the N-400

Country of Birth

Where were you born?

_____

Country of Nationality

Your country of nationality is the country or place where you are currently a citizen. If you are not currently a citizen anywhere, you can write *stateless*.

What is your country of nationality?

_____

Practice with a Partner
Ask and answer the questions.

Filling Out the N-400

Personal Information

The INS will ask you these questions.

Are either of your parents U.S. citizens? ☐ yes ☐ no

Some people with one or both U.S. citizen parents may already be U.S. citizens.

<table>
<tr>
<td>

┌─ Words to Know ─┐

current marital status
single
married
divorced
separated
widowed
annulled

</td>
<td>

What is your current marital status?

☐ **Single, Never Married** ☐ **Married**

☐ **Divorced** ☐ **Separated** ☐ **Widowed**

☐ **Marriage Annulled or Other**

</td>
</tr>
</table>

single, never married

married

divorced

widowed

Filling Out the N-400

Accommodations

Can you speak, read and write simple words and phrases in English?

❑ yes ❑ no

Do you know the basics of U.S. history and government?

❑ yes ❑ no

Most applicants must know English and basic U.S. history and government to become a citizen.

┌─ **Words to Know** ─┐
│ accommodation   │
│ disability   │
│ impairment   │
└──────────────────────┘

Are you requesting an accommodation in the naturalization process because of a disability or impairment ? ❑ yes ❑ no

If you answered yes, check the box below that names your disability or impairment.

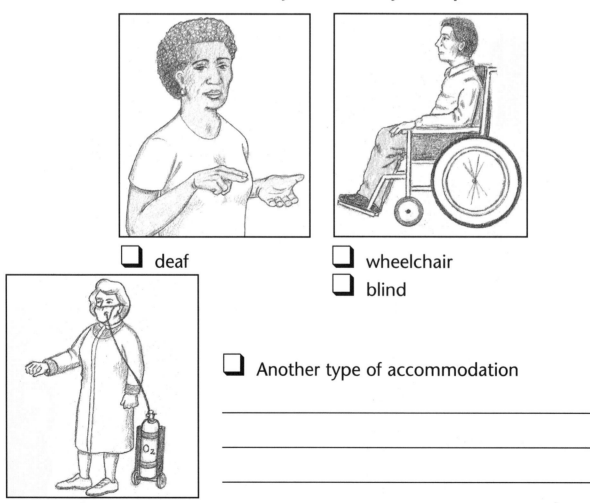

❑ deaf

❑ wheelchair
❑ blind

❑ Another type of accommodation

_____

_____

_____

Filling Out the N-400

Addresses and Telephone Numbers

The INS will ask you for this information. Do you know how to answer?

home address

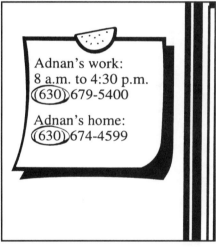

mailing address

apartment number

area code

daytime phone number

evening phone number

Addresses and Telephone Numbers

An ID = identification. A driver's license, a passport, and a green card are examples of IDs.

GEORGE H. RYAN SECRETARY OF STATE
NUMBER
M 236 6706 0000
BIRTHDATE
05-26-48
DRIVERS LICENSE

Adnan Murjedovic
617 S. Forest Ave. # 3
Rock Falls, IL 61071

SS# 123-45-6789

HT   WT   SEX
5 11   175   M

EXPIRES
05-26-06

ISSUED   CLASS   TYPE   ENDOR
09-07-02   *D*   REG   * * *
300000000

Adnan Murjedovic

ILLINOIS

Practice

Write your home address.

_____

Street number and name   Apartment number

_____

City   State   Zip Code

**Is your mailing address different from your home address?
If you answered yes, write your mailing address.**

_____

Street number and name, or PO Box   Apartment number

_____

City   State   Zip Code

Filling Out the N-400

Personal Information

The INS will ask you for some personal information. **Answer the questions.**

What is your sex?

 Male

 Female

What is your height?

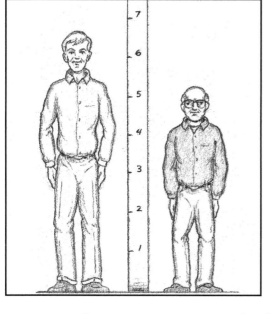

_____ feet _____ inches

one meter = more than 3 feet
  (39.37 inches)
one foot = 12 inches

What is your weight?

_____ pounds

one kilogram = 2.2 pounds

Personal Information

The INS may ask you for some more personal information. **Answer the questions.**

What is your race?
Check one box.

❑ White

❑ Asian or Pacific Islander

❑ Black

❑ Native American or Alaskan Native

❑ Other

What color is your hair?
Check one box.

❑ Black	❑ White
❑ Brown	❑ Red
❑ Blonde	❑ Sandy
❑ Gray	❑ Bald (No hair)

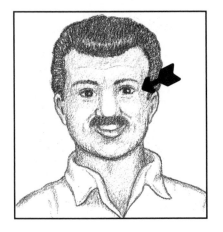

What color are your eyes?
Check one box.

❑ Brown	❑ Blue
❑ Green	❑ Hazel
❑ Gray	❑ Black
❑ Pink	❑ Maroon
❑ Other	

Dictation Practice

Some of the sentences in the dictation are about government and history. You will learn about them later in this book. Some are about everyday life.

Complete the sentences as your teacher reads.

1. I go to _____ every _____.

2. You work very _____ at your job.

3. _____ wanted to find a job.

4. They came to _____ in the United States.

5. I live in the _____ of _____.

Your teacher will say one of the words in each line. Circle the words you hear.

a.	we	see	She	me
b.	can	car	clean	council
c.	sit	speak	see	citizen
d.	east	eat	English	immigrant
e.	best	very	Virginia	vest
f.	well	with	went	west

Write the words you circled in order on the line to make a sentence.

_____

_____

Unit 2 Review

Draw a line from each INS question to the correct answer.

INS Questions	Answers
What is your social security number?	May 21, 1945
What is your date of birth?	2534 N. Clarence, Apt. 2
How long have you been a permanent resident?	5 feet, 9 inches
Where were you born?	(312) 267-9090
What is your current marital status?	355-43-9852
Your correct mailing address is?	in Mexico
Tell me your telephone number, area code first.	5 years
How tall are you?	I am married.

Practice with a Partner
Ask and answer the questions.

Unit 3
TALKING MORE ABOUT YOURSELF

Starting Out

- What is happening in the picture?
- How does the INS officer feel?

At the Interview

It is important to be positive and confident at your interview no matter how the INS officer feels.

Look at the pictures. How do you think these INS officers feel?

Look at this picture. What do you think will happen next? Draw a picture.

Filling Out the N-400

┌─ **Words to Know** ─┐

current
past
present
└─────────────────┘

Present and Past Addresses

The INS may ask you where you have lived for the past 5 years. **Write the addresses in the chart. Put your current address first.**

Street Number and Name, City, State, Zip Code, Country	Dates (*Month/Year*) From	To

Practice with a Partner

Where do you live?
Where did you live before your current address?
What city do you live in? what state?
When did you come to . . . ?

Filling Out the N-400

Words to Know

current
employer
most recent
occupation = job

Present and Past Employment

The INS may ask you where you have worked or attended school for the past 5 years.
Write the information in the chart. Put your most recent employer or school first. If you have not worked or gone to school, write *None*.

Employer or School Name	Employer or School Address *(Street, City and State)*	Dates *(Month/Year)* From	To	Your Occupation

The INS officer may ask about your job in the interview.

What do you do?

You're not working now, are you?

Did you work in the past?

Practice with a Partner

Use the phrases below to talk about your job.

I am a . . . .

I work at . . . .

I've worked there for . . . .

I started in . . . .

I used to work at . . . .

I left in . . . .

33

Time Outside the United States

The INS will ask you these questions. Do you know how to answer?

How many total days did you spend outside the United States in the past 5 years?

_____ days

How many trips of 24 hours or more have you taken outside the United States in the past 5 years?

_____ trips

If you spent time outside the United States in the past 5 years, fill in the chart.

Date you left the United States (Month/Day/Year)	Date you returned to the United States (Month/Day/Year)	Did trip last 6 months or more?		Countries to which you traveled	Total days outside the United States
		❑ yes	❑ no		
		❑ yes	❑ no		
		❑ yes	❑ no		
		❑ yes	❑ no		
		❑ yes	❑ no		
		❑ yes	❑ no		

Understanding the Interview

Words to Know

how long = how much time

Time Outside the United States

The INS may ask you about any trips you took outside the United States since you became a permanent resident.

Have you taken any trips outside the United States since you became a permanent resident?

Yes.

When did you leave the United States?

I left on March 1, 1998.

What country did you visit?

the Dominican Republic

How long were you out of the U.S.? Was it more than six months?

No. I was out of the U.S. for 20 days.

What date did you return to the U.S.?

I returned to the U.S. on March 21, 1998.

Practice with a Partner

Ask and answer the questions.

Filling Out the N-400

Marital History

The INS will ask you about your marital history. **Answer the questions.**

How many times have you been married? (including annulled marriages) _Once_

If you have never been married, go to page 39.

If you are currently married, the INS may want to know about your spouse.

Spouse's Family Name   **Given Name**   **Middle name (if applicable)**

Garcia   _Felipe_   _Felipe Jesus Garcia_

Date of Birth (Month/Day/Year)

_02/05/1968_

Date of Marriage (Month/Day/Year)

_____

Spouse's Social Security Number

_____

Home Address—Street Number and Name   **Apartment Number**

_____   _____

City, State, Zip Code

_____

Filling Out the N-400

Is your spouse a U.S. citizen? ☑ yes ☐ no

If your spouse IS a U.S. citizen:

When did your spouse become a U.S. citizen?

☐ **At birth** ☑ **Other**

If you checked "other" answer these questions.

Date your spouse became a citizen
(Month/Day/Year) _____

Place your spouse became a citizen

_____

If your spouse is NOT a U.S. citizen:

Spouse's country of citizenship _____
Spouse's INS "A" number   A_____

Spouse's Immigration Status
☐ Lawful Permanent Resident   ☐ Other

If you or your current spouse were married before, the INS will ask these questions about any prior spouses.

Practice with a Partner

Are you currently married?
What is your husband's or wife's full name?
When did you get married?
Where was your spouse born?
Is your spouse a U.S. citizen?

Understanding the Interview

Marital History

Read the conversation.

INS Officer: Are you married?

Liam: No, I'm not. I'm divorced.

INS Officer: Can I see a certified divorce decree?

Liam: Yes. Here it is.

INS Officer: How many times have you been married?

Liam: Just once.

Practice with a Partner

Say your conversation. Ask and answer the questions.

Marriage Fraud

Did you get your green card through marriage? The INS officer wants to know you got married for love, not for a green card.

real marriage

marriage fraud

The INS officer may ask these questions. **How will you answer?**
Are you still married?
Why are you separated?
Why did you get divorced?
Did you marry just to get a green card?

Filling Out the N-400

Your Children

The INS officer may ask you about your children.

How many children do you have? _____ 1

If you have one or more children, fill in the chart. Under *Current Address*, write *with me* if they live with you, their street address and country if they are not living with you, or *deceased* or *missing* if they are deceased or missing.

Full Name of Son or Daughter	Date of Birth (Month/Day/Year)	INS "A" Number (if child has one)	Country of birth	Current Address (Street, City, State, and Country)
Garcia ERIK	09/05/96			

Practice with a Partner

Do you have children?
What are your children's names?
Your children are citizens, right?
Where were your children born?
Are any of your children deceased?

It's the Law

Write the names of all your children on the N-400. You may help them get a green card or U.S. citizenship.

Filling Out the N-400

Words to Know

claimed = said or wrote
overdue = late

General Questions

Here are some more things the INS will ask.
How will you answer?

Have you ever claimed in writing or in any way, to be a U.S. citizen?

Have you ever registered to vote in any election in the United States? Have you ever voted in any election in the United States?

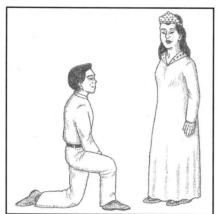

Were you born with (or do you have) any title of nobility in any foreign country?

Do you owe any federal, state, or local taxes that are overdue?

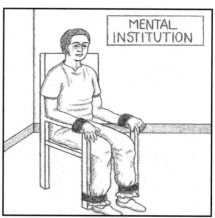

Have you ever been declared mentally incompetent?

If you answered *yes* to any of these questions, see a lawyer or legal expert.

Dictation Practice

These are common words in English.

Circle the words you already know.

the	to	is	was	of	a	he	she
that	for	and	in	it	you	on	as

Complete the sentences as your teacher reads.

1. The _____ was proud of her class.

2. _____ went to the _____ _____.

3. I _____ three _____.

4. The children _____ a television.

Your teacher will say one of the words in each line. Circle the word you hear.

a. I   is   it   if

b. where   want   why   won't

c. till   it   to   take

d. bill   back   begin   be

e. and   an   American   at

f. American   an   and   at

g. sit   see   citizen   council

Write the words you circled in order on the line to make a sentence.

_____

Unit 3 Review

Read the questions. Write the number of each question next to the correct word.

1. Where do you live?

2. Where do you work?

3. Have you spent time outside the United States since you became a permanent resident?

4. How many times have you been married?

5. Do you have any children?

6. Have you ever lied about being a U.S. citizen?

_____1_____ **Address**

_____5_____ **Children**

_____6_____ **Citizenship**

_____2_____ **Employment**

_____4_____ **Marriage**

_____3_____ **Trips**

Practice with a Partner

Ask and answer the questions.

Unit 4
BECOMING A CITIZEN

Preview

Find these things in the picture.

judge　　　new citizens　　　right hand

Starting Out

- Who are the people in this picture?
- What is happening?
- How do the people feel?

Warming Up

Talking Without Words

In the United States, if you look someone directly in the eyes, it shows you are honest. What does it mean in your country?

— Words to Know —

actions
confident
demanding
honest
nervous

Eye Contact

If you speak too softly, the officer may not understand you. If you act angry, the officer may get angry.

Tone of Voice

Filling Out the N-400

Words to Know

affiliations
communist
Nazi
persecuted

Affiliations

The INS will ask about your affiliations, the groups you have spent time with such as a church group or a soccer team.

Have you ever been a member of an organization in the United States or another place? If yes, write the name of the group below.

_____

Match the questions with the pictures. Write the number of the correct question in the box.

1. Have you ever been a member of the Communist party or any other totalitarian party or terrorist organization?

2. Have you ever advocated the overthrow of any government by force or violence?

3. Have you ever persecuted any person because of race, religion, national origin, or political opinion?

4. Between 1933 and 1945, were you a member of the Nazi Party, or did you help the Nazi government in any way?

Words to Know

failed to file
nonresident
tax return

Continuous Residence

The INS will ask you these questions about your resident status. **How will you answer?**

Since becoming a Lawful Permanent Resident of the United States:

Have you ever called yourself a nonresident on a federal, state, or local tax return?   ❑ yes   ❑ no

Note: Claiming to be a nonresident means that you live in another country.

Have you ever failed to file a federal, state, or local tax return because you thought you were a nonresident?
❑ yes   ❑ no

General Questions

You must not lie about your arrest record. The INS can find out about your arrests from your fingerprints, even if you use a different name.

Most traffic tickets are not arrests.

traffic tickets

You must tell the INS about an arrest for drunk driving. The INS officer may say you don't have good moral character if you were convicted of drunk driving. If you were arrested for drunk driving, see a lawyer.

drunk driving

You must tell the INS about being detained by a police officer or about being before a judge, and about all your arrests.

being detained by a police officer

being before a judge

Filling Out the N-400

Words to Know

arrested
convicted
detained
expunged = removed
guilty
innocent
probation
record

General Questions

If you want to be a U.S. citizen, you must tell the INS about all of your arrests.

The INS will ask these questions.
**How would the person in the picture answer?
Circle *yes* or *no*.**

1. Have you ever been arrested or detained by a police, military or INS officer for any reason? yes   no

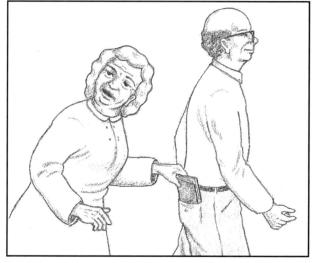

2. Have you ever committed a crime for which you were not arrested? yes   no

You are accused of committing a crime.

3. Have you ever been charged with committing any crime or offense? yes   no

4. Have you ever been convicted of a crime or offense?   yes   no

5. Have you ever been placed in alternative sentencing or rehabilitation program?   yes   no

6. Have you ever been in jail or prison?   yes   no

Practice with a Partner

Ask and answer the questions.
If you answered *yes* to any of the questions above, see a lawyer or legal counselor.

Words to Know

alimony
dependents
drunkard
gambling
habitual
prostitute

Good Moral Character Questions

Here are some more things the INS may ask about. **Match the questions with the pictures. Write the number of the correct question in the box.**

1. Have you ever been a habitual drunkard?

2. Have you ever paid anyone for sex or been paid as a prostitute?

3. Have you ever sold illegal drugs?

4. Have you ever had more than one wife or husband at the same time?
5. Did you ever help anyone enter the United States illegally?
6. Have you ever made a living from illegal gambling?
7. Have you ever failed to support your dependents or to pay alimony?

Removal, Exclusion, and Deportation

You must tell the INS about any deportation proceedings you have been through. **Answer the questions.**

Have you ever lied to any U.S. government official?

Are you currently involved in deportation or removal proceedings?

Have you ever been ordered deported or removed?

Have you ever been deported or removed from the United States?

Have you ever applied for suspension of deportation or removal?

Filling Out the N-400

Words to Know

deserted
exempted

U.S. Military Service

People who apply for citizenship must answer questions about military service.

Have you ever served in the U.S. military?

Have you ever left the United States so you would not be drafted?

Have you ever asked to be exempted from the U.S. military?

Have you ever deserted the U.S. military?

Practice with a Partner

Ask and answer the questions.

53

Selective Service Registration

SELECTIVE SERVICE REGISTRATION

NAME
ADDRESS
CITY   STATE   ZIP
PHONE   SS#

1
2
3
4
5

Selective Service Registration

Are you a male who lived in the United States between your 18th and 26th birthdays?
❑ yes ❑ no

If you answered *yes*, you need to answer the questions below.

Date Registered _____	Selective Service Number _____
Classification _____	Local Board Number _____

If you answered *yes*, but have not registered yet **and you are still under the age of 26,** you need to register for the Selective Service before you apply for naturalization.

If you answered *yes*, but have not registered yet **and you are now 26 years old or older,** the INS will ask you to write down why you did not register.

> I did not register for the Selective Service because I did not know about the requirement.
> Li Chen

What will you tell the INS?

Filling Out the N-400

Oath Requirements

To become a U.S. citizen, you must promise to support the Constitution. (See Unit 8.) You must also take an Oath of Allegiance to the United States. You must promise these things.

1. I believe in the Constitution and I will defend it.

2. I am not loyal to another government.

3. I will fight for the United States or help the army without fighting if the law says I have to.

4. I will work for the government in an emergency if the law says I have to.

5. I agree to this because I want to. I have no doubts or secret reasons.

You will be asked to sign your name to show that you understand and agree to everything in the oath.

I hereby certify, under penalty of perjury under the laws of the United States of America, that this application and the evidence submitted with it are all true and correct.

Signature _____ Date _____

Unit 4 Review

Circle *yes* or *no*.

1. Have you ever sold illegal drugs?   yes   (no)

2. Have you ever been an alcoholic?   yes   (no)

3. Have you ever practiced polygamy?   yes   (no)

4. Have you ever been arrested?   yes   (no)

5. Have you ever been a prostitute?   yes   (no)

6. Have you ever been declared mentally incompetent?   yes   (no)

It's the Law

If you answered *yes* to any of the questions above, you should talk with a lawyer before applying for citizenship.

Circle *yes* or *no*.

7. Will you take the oath of allegiance?   (yes)   no

8. Do you believe in the Constitution?   (yes)   no

9. Will you fight for America if required to?   (yes)   no

10. In a national emergency, will you work for the government

    if required to?   (yes)   no

It's the Law

If you answered *no* to any of the questions above, you should talk with a lawyer before applying for citizenship.

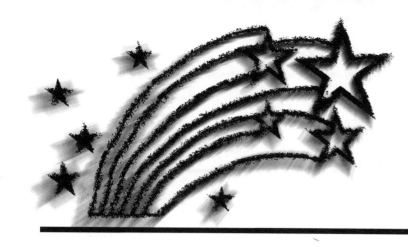

Unit 5

A NEW COUNTRY

The Thirteen Colonies

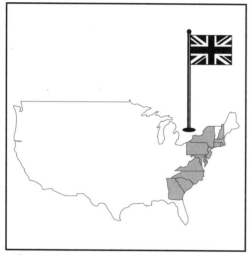

Independence

Revolution

Starting Out

- What is a colony?

- Was your native country ever a colony? If so, of what country?

- When did your country become independent?

Warming Up

Test Skills

You may take a multiple choice test to become a citizen. Multiple choice means that several answers are listed. You must choose the correct answer.

Sometimes one answer is obviously wrong. It could never be right.

Look at the example in the box. Which answer is obviously wrong?

Sometimes one answer is almost the same as the correct answer, but you know it is not correct. Look at the example. Which answer is almost the same as the correct answer?

Example

1. A multiple choice test gives you
   a. several answers
   b. one answer
   c. a blank to write on
   d. a telephone

Warming Up

Test Skills

When you are thinking about how to answer, ignore the answers that you know are not correct.

Example

2. How many years is a Senator's term?
   a. one year
   b. two years
   c. six years
   d. ten years

In the example, you know the answer isn't **b** or **d**, so it must be **a** or **c**. Read **a** and **c** again. C is the correct answer.

Always answer every question. If a question is hard, write a dot next to it. You can go back and do it later.

If you have no idea of what an answer is, guess. You may be correct.

History: The New World

Ready to Read

How did you come to the United States?

on foot   by boat

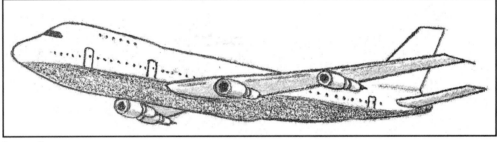

by plane

When did you come to the United States?

Why did you come to the United States?

Practice with a Partner
Ask and answer the questions.

_____

The Statue of Liberty was a gift from France in 1876. Now she welcomes all immigrants who come to the United States.

History: The New World

Coming to America

Before the United States was a colony or country, Native Americans had lived here a long time.

Christopher Columbus sailed from Spain to America in 1492. **Draw an arrow ➡ from Spain to America.**

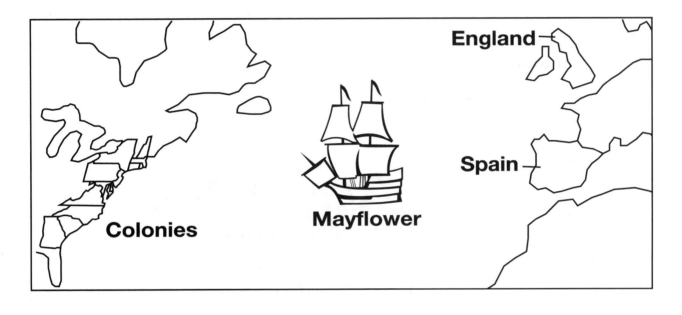

More than 125 years later, a group of Pilgrims sailed from England to America. They came on a ship called the Mayflower. **Circle the Mayflower.**

The Pilgrims came to America for religious freedom. They started a colony. The colony belonged to England. **Put a cross ✚ on the colonies.**

The Pilgrims and Thanksgiving

The Pilgrims arrived in America in the winter. They had no food. Many of them died.

The Native Americans (American Indians) helped the Pilgrims to plant food and build houses.

The next fall, the Pilgrims and the Indians had a big dinner called Thanksgiving. The Pilgrims gave thanks for the help.

NOVEMBER

S	M	T	W	TH	F	S
1	2	3	4	5	6	7
8	9	10	11	12	13	14
15	16	17	18	19	20	21
22	23	24	25	26	27	28
29	30					

Now we celebrate Thanksgiving on the fourth Thursday of November. **Circle Thanksgiving on the calendar.**

History

The Revolutionary War and Independence

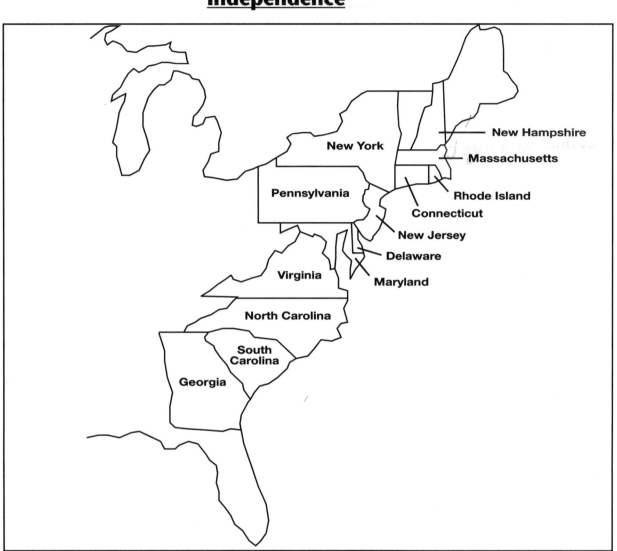

Words to Know

coast
original

By 1770 England had 13 colonies on the east coast of North America. These colonies became the original 13 states.

Practice

Have you visited any original states? Which ones?
Which colonies begin with the letter M?
Which colonies begin with the letter N?
Which colonies begin with the letter A?

History

The Revolutionary War and Independence

Words to Know

rule
colonist
laws
liberty
taxes
trade
protest

The King of England ruled the colonies. Many colonists didn't like English laws. The colonists didn't want to pay high taxes to England. They wanted to trade with other countries. But the King said, "You must pay the taxes. You must trade only with England."

The colonists got angry. They protested. At a meeting Patrick Henry said, "Give me liberty or give me death."

The Revolutionary War and Independence

Words to Know

leader
independence
equal
representatives

The colonists' protest became a revolution. A revolution is a war against the government.

Thomas Jefferson was a leader of the colonists. He wrote a letter to the king. This letter is called the Declaration of Independence.

The Declaration of Independence says "All men are created equal" and have the right to "life, liberty, and the pursuit of happiness." The colonists wanted their own government independent of England.

On July 4, 1776, representatives from the 13 colonies signed the Declaration of Independence.

The Revolution and Independence

The Revolutionary War lasted eight years, from 1775 to 1783.

The leader, or commander in chief, of the colonial (American) army was George Washington.

The American army won the war. England lost. The United States became independent. Now we celebrate Independence Day on the 4th of July, the birthday of the United States.

George Washington became the first president of the United States. He is called the "Father of Our Country." His picture is on the one dollar bill and on the quarter.

Martha Washington was the first president's wife. She was the first First Lady.

Practice with a Partner

When is Independence Day in your country?

Does your country have a "father"?

What is his name?

Passing the Test

Test Skills

The test and the interview include questions that begin with these words:

> Who   What   When   Where   Why

Each question word helps you know how to answer.

1. The answer to "What?" is often the name of a person or thing.

   What did the colonists plant?

   What is your name?

2. The answer to "Who?" is a person.

   Who was the first president?

   Who came with you to the interview?

3. The answer to "When?" is a time or date.

   When do we celebrate Independence Day?

   When were you born?

4. The answer to "Where?" is a place.

   Where were the 13 colonies?

   Where were you born?

5. The answer to "Why?" is a reason.

   Why did the Pilgrims come to America?

   Why do you want to become a citizen?

Practice with a Partner

Ask and answer the questions.

Dictation Practice

Some of the test answers may be used in the dictation.

Complete the sentences as your teacher reads.

1. George ___washington___ was the first ___President___.

2. All people want to be ___Free___.

3. ___AMERICA___ is the land of the ___Free___.

4. Many ___people___ have ___djed___ for freedom.

5. Martha ___Washington___ was
   the first ___First___ ___Lady___.

The Test

Circle the correct answer.

1. Why did the Pilgrims come to America?
   a. to buy more land
   b. to escape sickness
   c. for religious freedom
   d. none of the above

2. Who helped the Pilgrims in America?
   a. the American Indians
   b. the Spanish
   c. the English
   d. the Africans

3. What holiday was celebrated for the first time by the American colonists?
   a. Christmas
   b. Thanksgiving
   c. Labor Day
   d. May Day

4. What do we celebrate on the 4th of July?
   a. Washington's Birthday
   b. Independence Day
   c. Lincoln's Birthday
   d. Thanksgiving

5. What country did America fight in the Revolutionary War?
   a. France
   b. Germany
   c. England
   d. Japan

6. The first President of the United States was George Washington.
   a. Thomas Jefferson
   b. Patrick Henry
   c. George Washington
   d. Abraham Lincoln

7. Who was the main writer of the Declaration of Independence?
   a. Thomas Jefferson
   b. Patrick Henry
   c. George Washington
   d. Abraham Lincoln

8. The basic belief of the Declaration of Independence is
   a. Give me liberty or give me death.
   b. The King has supreme power.
   c. No more taxes.
   d. All men are created equal.

9. When was the Declaration of Independence adopted?
   a. 1985
   b. 1783
   c. 1492
   d. 1776

10. What were the 13 original states of the U.S. called?
    a. capitals
    b. prefectures
    c. colonies
    d. provinces

11. Which president was the first commander-in-chief of the U.S. army and navy?
    a. George Washington
    b. Patrick Henry
    c. Thomas Jefferson
    d. Abraham Lincoln

12. Who said, "Give me liberty or give me death!"
    a. Abraham Lincoln
    b. Thomas Jefferson
    c. George Washington
    d. Patrick Henry

13. Massachusetts is one of the 13 original colonies.
    a. Michigan
    b. Massachusetts
    c. Indiana
    d. California

14. What is the date of Independence Day?
    a. December 25
    b. November 12
    c. July 4
    d. None of the above

15. Independence from whom?
    a. Italy
    b. Japan
    c. Germany
    d. England

16. Which president is called "the father of our country?"
    a. Thomas Jefferson
    b. Abraham Lincoln
    c. Bill Clinton
    d. George Washington

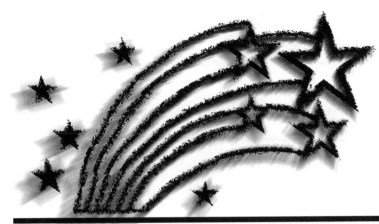

Unit 6
THE CIVIL WAR AND EXPANSION

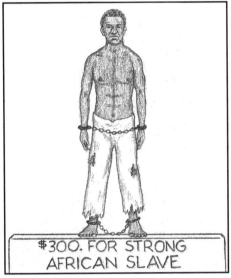

$300. FOR STRONG AFRICAN SLAVE

slavery

Civil War

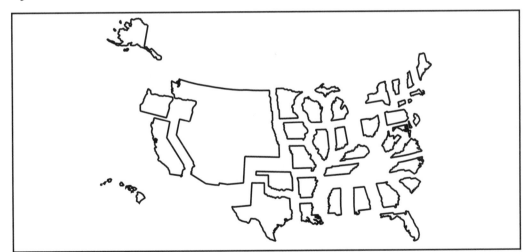

U.S. Expansion: The United States Today

Starting Out

- What do the words **slavery**, **Civil War** and **expansion** mean?

- Did your native country ever have slavery?

- Was there a civil war in your country?

Warming Up

Remembering

To study for the test, you must memorize the answer to the test questions. Memorize means "to remember." People memorize answers in different ways.

1. Think of a picture.

This one says George Washington was the first President of the United States.

Practice

What does this picture say?

2. Use the first letters of the words.

Practice

What do the first letters of these words help you remember?

Slaves   South

Remembering

3. Use music or poetry.

These help us to remember that there are stars and stripes on the flag, and the date that Columbus sailed to America from Spain.

4. Associate the idea with numbers.

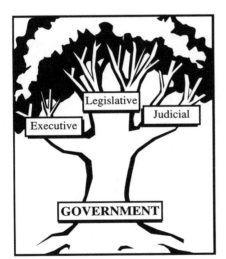

This picture reminds us that the government has three parts, or branches. See page 104.

Survey

How many people in your class have tried:

pictures _____   first letters _____   singing _____

associations _____ poetry _____

Which way do you like best? Why?

History

Words to Know

captured
free
slave

The Civil War

After the Revolutionary War, some people in the United States still were not free. In 1860 one of every seven Americans was a slave.

Many slaves were from Africa. They were captured and brought to the United States. Then they were sold to people who wanted workers. Slaves worked many hours without pay.

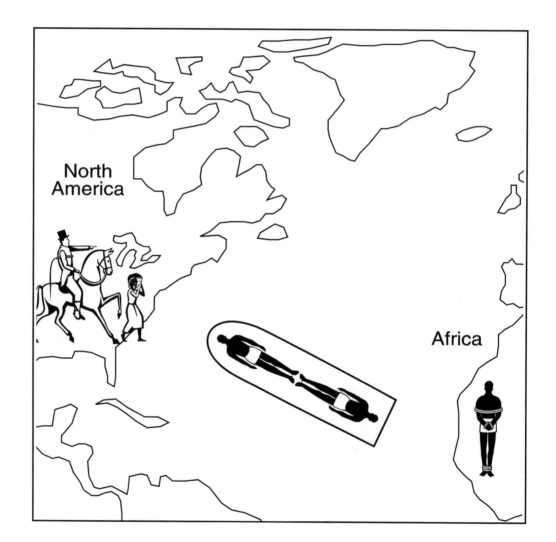

Practice

Put an x on Africa.
Circle the slave ship.
Draw a box around the slave in the United States.
Draw a star on the United States.

History

Words to Know

Confederacy
factories
farm
illegal
slavery
Union

The Civil War

By 1860 there were many differences between the northern and the southern states. The North had many factories. Slavery was illegal in the North. The South had mostly farms. Many slaves worked on small and large farms in the South. Large farms were called plantations.

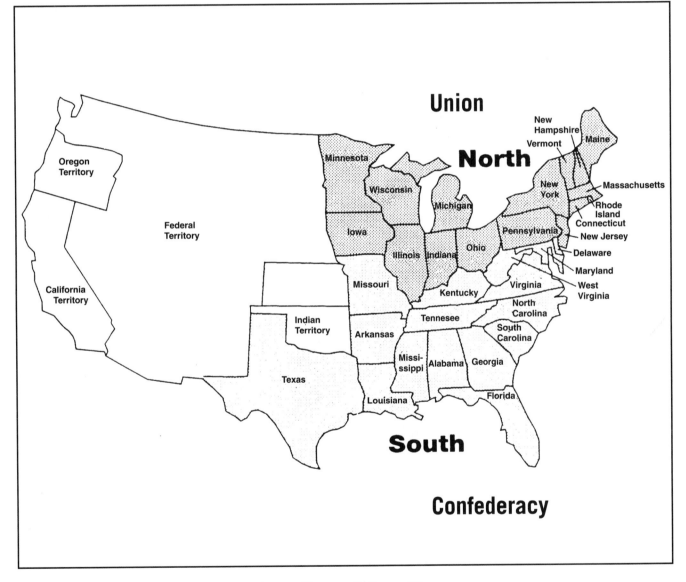

Practice with a Partner

Was your state in the North?
Was your state in the South?
Was your state a part of the United States in 1860?

History

Words to Know

Confederacy
separate
Union
unite

The Civil War

The South thought that the U.S. government did not represent them. They decided to form their own country, the Confederacy. The North did not want to separate. The U.S. government formed the Union Army in the North to unite the country.

The Civil War lasted from 1861-1865. Many people from both sides died.

Practice

Match the words with the pictures.

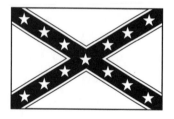

slavery

Confederacy

illegal

History

The Civil War

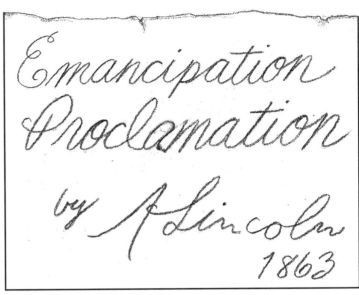

Words to Know

Abraham Lincoln
Emancipation Proclamation

The President of the United States during the Civil War was Abraham Lincoln. He was against slavery. He freed most of the slaves in a document called the Emancipation Proclamation.

Practice with a Partner

Who was Abraham Lincoln?
What did he do?
What is the Emancipation Proclamation?

freed the slaves.

The Civil War

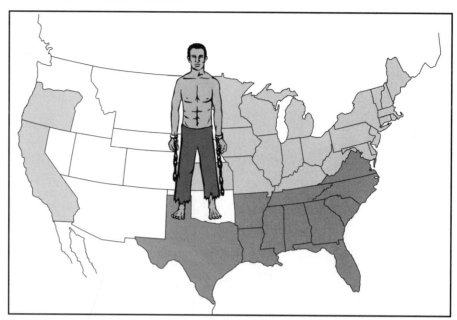

The North won the Civil War in 1865. The North and South became one country again. Soon after the war, Lincoln was killed.

Abraham Lincoln
1865

Words to Know

amendment = change to the Constitution, see pages 103 and 104.
Constitution = the supreme law of the United States, (see page 102.)

FREE
Article 1
Article 2
Article 3

In 1865 the 13th amendment was added to the Constitution. It ended slavery forever.

Practice with a Partner

When did the Civil War end?
Who won?
What did the 13th Amendment do?

History: Expansion

The United States quickly grew from the 13 original states to 50!

The government bought land from France and Spain in the early 1800s.

Later, the United States took over Texas.

The United States won California and most of the southwest in a war with Mexico.

England gave the United States the northwest states.

History: Expansion

Russia sold the United States Alaska, the 49th state.

+

The United States took control of Hawaii, the 50th state of the Union, in 1898.

=

The United States now has 50 states.

History: The American Flag

Reading for the Test

The first American flag was made by Betsy Ross during the Revolutionary War. It had six white stripes, seven red stripes, and thirteen white stars, one for each colony. Each time a new state was added to the United States, a white star was added to the blue field in the corner. There are now fifty stars on the flag, one for each state.

Practice

Circle the picture that tells about the word.

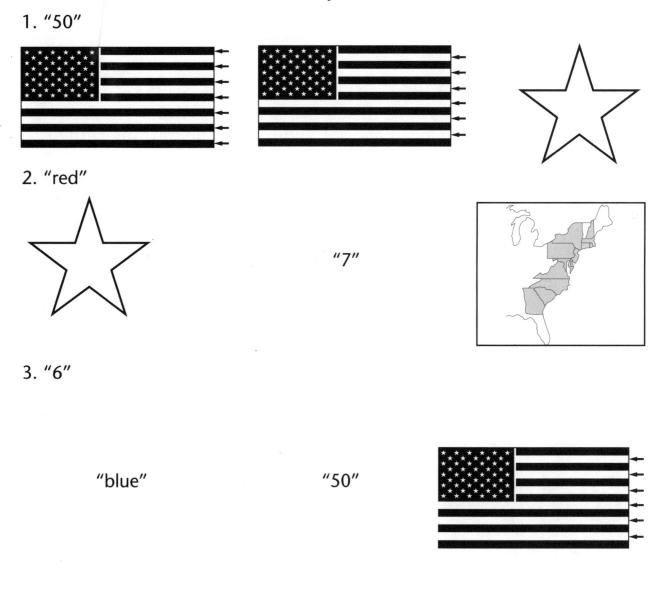

1. "50"

2. "red"

"7"

3. "6"

"blue"

"50"

History: The American National Anthem

In 1812 the English navy attacked a U.S. fort. Francis Scott Key watched the attack. Because it was dark, he did not know who won. The next morning he saw the American flag still flying over the fort; the United States had won.

escribió

Nombre Himno Nacional

Francis Scott Key wrote a poem about this called the "Star Spangled Banner." It is now the U.S. national anthem.

Words to Know

anthem = song
banner = flag
dawn = early morning
perilous = dangerous

Practice

Circle these words in the poem: **flag, star, stars, stripes, Star Spangled Banner.**

Oh say, can you see, by the dawn's early light,
What so proudly we hailed at the twilight's last gleaming?
Whose broad stripes and bright stars
through the perilous fight,
O'er the ramparts we watched, were so gallantly streaming!
And the rockets red glare, the bombs bursting in air,
Gave proof through the night that our flag was still there.
Oh say, does that star spangled banner yet wave
O'er the land of the free and the home of the brave?

Practice with a Partner

Have you heard the "Star Spangled Banner"? Where?
Does your country have a national anthem? What is it called?

Dictation Practice

If you learn an answer for the test, you have learned a sentence for the dictation part of the test.

Complete the sentences as your teacher reads.

1. The colors of the _____ are red, _____,

   and _____.

2. The American flag has _____ and _____.

3. The American flag has 13 _____.

4. The flag of the United States has 50 _____.

Write the sentences as your teacher reads.

1. _____

2. _____

The Test

Circle the correct answer.

1. Who was the president during the Civil War?
   a. George Washington
   b. Patrick Henry
   (**c.**) Abraham Lincoln
   d. Thomas Jefferson

2. What amendment to the Constitution freed the slaves?
   a. 13th
   b. 18th
   c. 1st
   d. none of the above

   NO

3. Which President freed the slaves?
   a. Patrick Henry
   b. George Washington
   (**c.**) Abraham Lincoln
   d. Thomas Jefferson

4. What did the Emancipation Proclamation do?
   (**a.**) freed many slaves
   b. gave women the vote
   c. declared war against the south
   d. declared independence from England

5. What was the Southern Army called?
   a. the Union
   b. the Confederacy
   c. the Allies
   d. the Communists

   No

6. What is the 49th state in the Union?
   (**a.**) Alaska
   b. Hawaii
   c. New York
   d. California

7. __Hawaii__ is the 50th state in the Union.
   (**a.**) Hawaii
   b. Alaska
   c. New York
   d. California

8. What are the colors of our flag?
   a. red, white, and green
   b. purple, yellow, and red
   c. blue, yellow, and green
   (**d.**) red, white, and blue

9. What do the stars on the flag mean?
   (**a.**) one for each state in the union.
   b. one for each year as a colony.
   c. one for each colony.
   d. none of the above.

10. How many stripes are there on the flag?
    a. 50
    (**b.**) 13
    c. 25
    d. 4

11. How many stars are there on our flag?
    a. 13
    b. 25
    c. 4
    d. 50

12. What color are the stars on our flag?
    a. blue
    b. red
    c. white
    d. green

13. What do the stripes on the flag mean?
    a. They represent 13 years.
    b. They represent the original 13 colonies.
    c. They represent the original 50 states.
    d. none of the above.

14. What color are the stripes?
    a. blue and red
    b. white and blue
    c. green and yellow
    d. red and white

15. How many states are there in the Union?
    a. 13
    b. 100
    c. 26
    d. 50

16. What is the national anthem of the United States?
    a. The Star Spangled Banner
    b. The Capitol
    c. The White House
    d. The Revolutionary War

17. Who wrote the Star Spangled Banner?
    a. George Washington
    b. Abraham Lincoln
    c. Francis Scott Key
    d. Martin Luther King

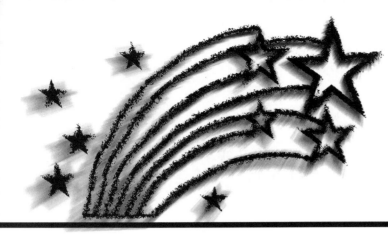

Unit 7
THE 20TH CENTURY AND VOTING

World War II (1941–1945)

Civil Rights Movement (1960)

Starting Out

Many countries fought in World War II.

• Did your country fight?

The U.S. Civil Rights Movement helped many people to vote.

• Can all people adults in your native country?

• Did you vote in your country? Why or why not?

Warming Up

Studying for the Test

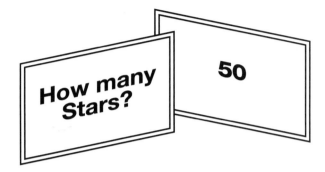

Some people make flash cards.

Some people post information where they will read it many times during the day.

Some people study quietly alone. Others need music and people.

Survey

How many people in your class study:

1. alone? _____

2. with someone? _____

3. in the morning? _____

4. in the evening? _____

5. at home? _____

6. with notes? _____

History: World War II

Words to Know

Allies
enemies
freedom

Reading for the Test

The United States fought for freedom in many wars during the 20th century. In 1941 the United States entered World War II, the largest war in history. More than 22 million people died!

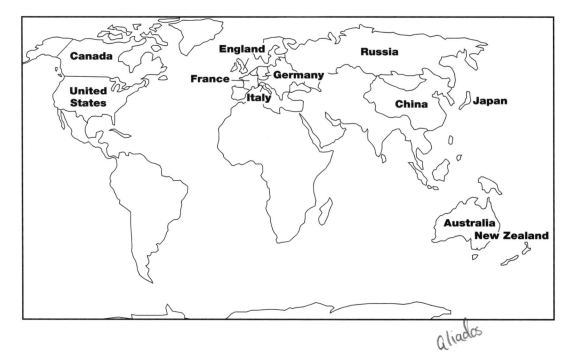

aliados

The United States joined the Allies (France, England, Russia, Canada, China, Australia, and New Zealand). The Allies fought against our enemies, the Axis: Japan, Italy, Germany, and other countries. The war ended in 1945 after the United States dropped two atomic bombs on Japan.

Practice

1. Put an x on Japan, Italy, and Germany.

2. Circle the Allies.

The United Nations

Words to Know

resolve world problems
economic aid =

$10,000

The United Nations was formed after World War II to discuss and try to resolve world problems and to provide economic aid to many countries.

Practice with a Partner

Is your native country a member of the United Nations?

Has the United Nations helped your country? How?

History: The Civil Rights Movement

Reading for the Test

Words to Know

civil rights
discriminatory
equality
non-violent
protest

After World War II, the United States still faced a threat to freedom at home: segregation. Segregation is the separation of people because of skin color. In the 1960s many people protested against segregation. They wanted all people to have equality.

Martin Luther King, Jr. was a famous civil rights leader. He worked for equality.

He led many non-violent marches to change discriminatory laws.

History: The Civil Rights Movement

In 1968, Martin Luther King, Jr. was shot and killed. Because of the Civil Rights Movement, there are now many laws to stop discrimination. We celebrate Martin Luther King's birthday on the third Monday in January.

Practice

Match the word with the picture.

protest

discriminatory

equality

non-violent

The Right to Vote

The right to vote is the most important right of U.S. citizens. Many Americans have fought for the freedom to vote. Martin Luther King, Jr. fought against discriminatory laws that made it difficult for Black people to vote in some states.

Civics

Words to Know

minimum
voter registration
serious criminal convictions

Voting Requirements

To legally vote in the United States, you must:

be 18 years old.

be a U.S. citizen (If you were not born a U.S. citizen, you must have received your naturalization certificate.)

Voter's Identification Card
LaPorte County Indiana

Name

Address

Ward   Pct.   Reg. No.

I hereby certify that the above name elector was registered as a voter of LaPorte County on   and now resides in the Ward and precinct indicated.

_____Bd. of Reg. Officer
_____Dep. Reg. Officer
_____Sig. of Voter

be registered to vote.

have no serious criminal convictions.

The minimum voting age in the United States is 18 years old.
You must register (fill out a form) if you want to vote.
Note: North Dakota does not require voter registration.

Practice with a Partner

How do you register to vote in your state?

Civics

Voting and Citizenship

As a citizen, you can make you voice heard through your vote. Citizens can elect representatives to speak for them in federal, state, and local government. Voting is the most important right of U.S. citizens.

Citizens of the U.S. have many benefits.

U.S. citizens can...

vote.

JOB APPLICATION
US POSTAL SERVICE

apply for federal jobs.

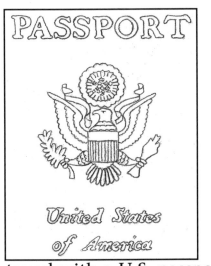

travel with a U.S. passport.

serve on a jury.

Why do you think voting is the most important right of U.S. citizens?

Civics

How to Vote

In the United States there are two main political parties: the Democrats and the Republicans. Members of political parties do not agree on everything, but they often share many ideas.

Practice with a Partner

What do you know about Democrats and Republicans?
What politicians are Democrats?
What politicians are Republicans?

In primary elections people choose one candidate from each political party. The winners represent their political party in the final election, called the general election.

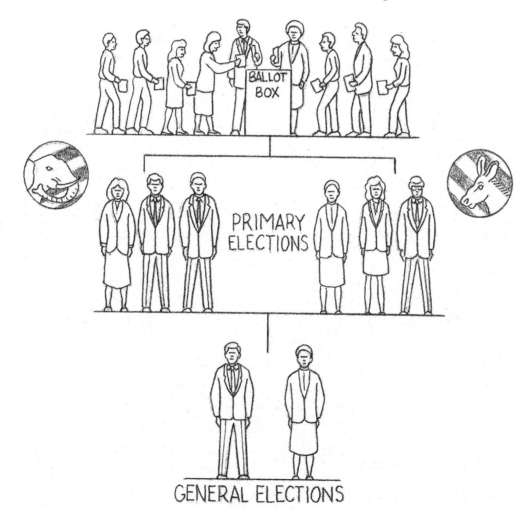

Civics

Words to Know

campaign
endorsement
special interest group

Learning About the Candidates

Before you vote, learn about the different political offices and the candidates for each office. There are many ways you can learn.

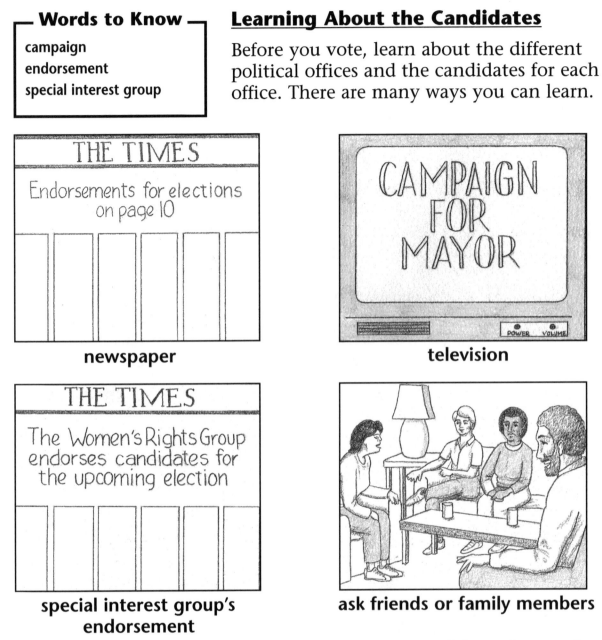

THE TIMES

Endorsements for elections on page 10

newspaper

CAMPAIGN FOR MAYOR

POWER   VOLUME

television

THE TIMES

The Women's Rights Group endorses candidates for the upcoming election

special interest group's endorsement

ask friends or family members

Are there any other ways you can learn about candidates for an election?

Survey

How many people in class...

1. will vote as a U.S. citizen? _____

2. read about politics in the newspaper? _____

3. talk to friends or family about politics? _____

4. would like to be an elected official? _____

Practice

Put a check next to the names of our Allies during World War II.

____ United States	____ Mexico	____ Russia	____ Germany
____ New Zealand	____ Italy	____ Japan	____ France
____ Australia	____ Canada	____ England	____ China

Practice

Match the picture with the citizenship benefit.

serve on a jury

travel with a U.S. passport

vote

apply for federal jobs

Dictation Practice

Capital letters are big letters that begin words describing important people, places, or things. Every sentence begins with a capital letter.

Write your name.

_____

Circle the capital letters in your name.

Write the sentences below with the correct capitals.

1. citizens have the right to vote. _____

_____

2. i want to become an american so i can vote. _____

_____

3. america fought for freedom in world war ii.

_____

_____

4. martin luther king, jr was a famous civil rights leader.

_____

_____

Write the sentences as your teacher reads.

1. _____

_____

2. _____

_____

The Test

Circle the correct answer.

1. What is the minimum voting age in the United States?
   a. 16
   b. 18 *(circled)*
   c. 20
   d. 21

2. What are the two major political parties in the United States?
   a. Legislative and Executive
   b. President and Vice President
   c. Democrat and Republican *(circled)*
   d. Constitution and Bill of Rights

3. Name one purpose *proposito* of the United Nations.
   a. to discuss world problems *(circled)*
   b. to vote for president
   c. to fight wars
   d. to serve on a jury

4. Which countries were our allies during World War II?
   a. Germany, Japan, and Italy
   b. France, England, and Russia *(circled)*
   c. Mexico, El Salvador, and Guatemala
   d. Cambodia, Vietnam, and Laos

5. Who was Martin Luther King, Jr.?
   a. the second president
   b. father of our country
   c. a civil rights leader *(circled)*
   d. a pilgrim

6. What is the most important right granted to U.S. citizens?
   a. right to vote *(circled)*
   b. right to serve on a jury
   c. right to apply for federal jobs
   d. right to smile

7. Name one benefit of being a U.S. citizen.
   a. right to vote
   b. right to serve on a jury
   c. right to apply for federal jobs
   d. all of the above *(circled)*

8. Which countries were our enemies during World War II?
   a. Germany, Italy, and France
   b. Germany, China, and the Soviet Union
   c. Iraq, Libya, and Saudi Arabia
   d. Germany, Italy, and Japan *(circled)*

Unit 8
THE U.S. CONSTITUTION AND THE BILL OF RIGHTS

Preview

Find these things in the pictures.

police officer   gun   judge   lawyer

Starting Out

- What is a law? Give an example.
- What rule or law did the man in the picture break?
- Are the laws in the United States the same as in your country? How are they the same or different? Give an example.

Warming Up

Dictation Preparation

Words and Phrases with *the*

the United States
the Fourth of July
the White House
the capital
the Declaration of
   Independence
the House of
   Representatives
the Bill of Rights

the American people
the American flag
the Senate
the President
the Constitution
the Revolutionary War
the Supreme law of
   the land

Words and Phrases without *the*

America
July 4th
Congress

freedom
Washington, D.C.

Dictation Tip

Short words can be hard to hear. One of these words is *the*. Try to learn common phrases with *the*.

Practice

Look at the list above. Then fill in the blanks below with *the*. Remember: some words are without *the*. Put an X in those blanks.

1. _____ White House is in _____ Washington, D.C.

2. On _____ July 4th we celebrate _____ American independence.

3. _____ Congress is made up of _____ Senate and _____

   House of Representatives.

4. _____ Bill of Rights protects people's _____ freedom.

5. _____ Constitution was written after _____ Revolutionary War.

The Constitution, the Highest Law

Words to Know

supreme   state
federal   local

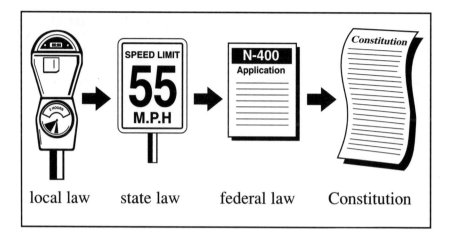

local law   state law   federal law   Constitution

Reading for the Test

Look at the picture. Read about the Constitution.

The Constitution is the supreme law of the land. It is the highest law in the United States. All laws must agree with the Constitution. There are three kinds of laws: **federal** laws (laws for all of the states), **state** laws (laws for each of the states), and **local** laws (laws for a city, town, or village).

Immigration laws are federal laws. Driving laws are state laws. Parking laws are local laws.

Find and Write

Find the information, then write it below.

A federal law	
A state law	
A local law	

Parts of the Constitution

Reading for the Test
Look at the pictures. Then read about the Constitution.

Philadelphia

⎡ Words to Know ⎤
preamble
articles
amendments

In 1787, representatives from the new states met in Philadelphia, Pennsylvania. They wrote the U.S. Constitution—the plan of the U.S. government.

The Constitution has three parts: the **preamble**, the 7 **articles**, and the 27 **amendments**.

| Preamble (introduction) | → | 7 articles (form of government) | → | 27 Amendments (changes) |

Parts of the Constitution

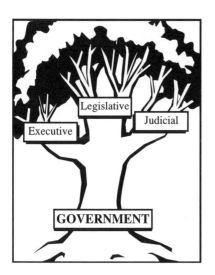

Reading for the Test

Read about the parts of the Constitution.

The Preamble

The Preamble is the introduction to the Constitution. Here are the first words of the Preamble:

We, the People of the United States...

The Seven Articles

The Articles talk about the **form** of the government. The government has three **branches**.

Executive
President
Vice President
Cabinet

Legislative
Senators
Representatives

Judicial
Supreme Court
Federal Courts

The Amendments

Changes, or *amendments*, were added to the Constitution. There are 27 amendments.

The Bill of Rights

Reading for the Test

Read about the Bill of Rights.

The first ten **amendments** were added to the Constitution in 1791. These amendments are called the Bill of Rights. The Constitution and the Bill of Rights **guarantee**, or protect, the rights of all people living in the United States. They protect citizens and non-citizens.

The First Amendment guarantees, or protects, these rights:

Match the freedom with the picture. Write the number on the line.

  _3_ Freedom of religion

  _2_ Freedom of speech

  _1_ Freedom of the press

  _5_ Freedom to assemble peacefully

  _4_ Freedom to ask for a change in the government

The Bill of Rights

Take a Look

Look at the pictures below. Do you know what rights they show?

Practice with a Partner

Are these rights in the First Amendment? Circle yes or no.

yes   no

yes   no

yes   no

yes   no

I will **not** answer any questions.

yes   no

The Bill of Rights

Reading for the Test

Look at the pictures. What right does each amendment give?

2nd Amendment

3rd Amendment

4th Amendment

I will not answer any questions.

5th Amendment

Words to Know

force	testify
property	tried
search	

Match the sentence with the picture. Write the number of the amendment next to the sentence.

___4/th___ The government must have a warrant (an order from a court) to search or take a person's property.

___2nd___ You have the right to bear arms (own a gun).

___5th___ A person doesn't have to testify against himself or herself.

___3rd___ The government cannot force you to keep soldiers in your home when there is no war.

The Bill of Rights

Reading for the Test

Look at the pictures. What rights do these amendments give?

6th Amendment

7th Amendment

8th Amendment

9th Amendment

10th Amendment

Words to Know

jury
power
represented
trial

Match the sentence with the picture. Write the number of the amendment next to the sentence.

__8th__ The court cannot give a person cruel punishment or an excessive fine (a fine that is too high).

__6th__ A person charged with a crime has the right to a trial and to be represented by a lawyer. licensed

__9th__ The people have rights that are not written in the Constitution.

__10th__ The people or the states have any power that is not given to the federal government in the Constitution.

__7th__ In many cases a person has the right to a trial by jury.

Voting Rights Amendments

Take a Look

Look at the pictures. How are they the same? How are they different?

Four amendments protect people's right to vote. Read each amendment.

15th Amendment (1870):
Men of all races can vote.

19th Amendment (1920):
Women can vote.

24th Amendment (1964):
No one has to pay a tax to vote.

26th Amendment (1971):
Any citizen 18 years and older can vote.

Practice

Draw a line from the question to the answer.

INS Questions	Answers
What is the Constitution?	1787
In what year was it written?	The first ten amendments to the Constitution
What is the Bill of Rights?	Freedom of speech
Name one right guaranteed by the First Amendment.	The supreme law of the land

Write the questions and answers. Copy the language above.

Q: What is _____?

A: _____

Q: In what _____?

A: _____

Q: What is _____?

A: _____

Q: Name one _____.

_____

A: _____

Dictation Practice

Some dictation sentences need commas.
Commas are used between dates (day, year) and
places (city, state).

July 4, 1776 (**date**)   Philadelphia, Pennsylvania (**place**)

1. What city and state do you live in? _____

Circle the comma between your city and state.

2. When is your birthday? _____

Circle the comma between the day and year.

3. What is the capital of the United States? _____

Circle the comma between the city and state.

4. When is Independence Day? _____
Circle the comma between the day and year.

Your teacher will say some sentences that need commas. Write them below.

1. _____

2. _____

The Test

Circle the correct answer.

1. What is the Constitution?
   a. a local law
   b. the colonies
   c. a right
   (d.) the supreme law of the land

2. What are three rights or freedoms guaranteed by the Bill of Rights?
   a. love, peace, and justice
   (b.) speech, religion, and press
   c. legislative, executive, and judicial
   d. preamble, articles, and amendments

3. What do we call a change to the Constitution?
   (a.) an amendment
   b. the preamble
   c. a branch of government
   d. a right

4. What are the three branches of our government?
   a. love, peace, and justice
   b. speech, religion, and press
   (c.) legislative, executive, and judicial
   d. preamble, articles, and amendments

5. Where does freedom of speech come from?
   a. the Declaration of Independence
   b. the Articles of the Constitution
   c. the flag
   (d.) the Bill of Rights

6. What is the introduction to the Constitution called?
   (a.) the Preamble
   b. the Amendments
   c. the Articles
   d. the President

7. What are the first ten amendments to the Constitution called?
   a. the 27 amendments
   b. independence
   (c.) the Bill of Rights
   d. freedom of speech

8. Name one amendment that guarantees or addresses voting rights.
   a. 1st
   b. 2nd
   c. 4th
   (d.) 19th

9. In what year was the Constitution written?
   a. 1776
   b. 1865
   (c.) 1787
   d. 1920

10. Whose rights are guaranteed by the U.S. Constitution and the Bill of Rights?
    a. U.S. citizens
    b. everyone in the United States
    c. Mexican citizens
    d. everyone in the world

11. Name one right guaranteed by the First Amendment.
    a. the right to vote
    b. the right to a trial by jury
    c. the right to free speech
    d. the right to freedom (no slavery)

12. Can the Constitution be changed?
    a. yes
    b. until 1787
    c. no
    d. every 25 years

13. How many branches are in our government?
    a. one
    b. two
    c. three
    d. four

14. How many changes or amendments are there to the Constitution?
    a. 10
    b. 15
    c. 23
    d. 27

15. What is the supreme law of the land?
    a. the Congress
    b. the President
    c. the Constitution
    d. the amendments

16. Which of these is guaranteed by the First Amendment?
    a. freedom of the press
    b. the right to bear arms
    c. the right to a trial by jury in most cases
    d. the right to a job

17. Which of the following amendments to the Constitution does not guarantee or address voting rights?
    a. the 5th Amendment
    b. the 15th Amendment
    c. the 19th Amendment
    d. the 24th Amendment

18. Which list contains three rights or freedoms guaranteed by the Bill of Rights?
    a. freedom of religion, the right to vote, and the right to a trial by jury
    b. freedom of life, freedom of justice, and freedom of happiness
    c. freedom of speech, freedom of the press, and freedom of religion
    d. the right to a job, the right to eat, and the right to a house

Unit 9
THE LEGISLATIVE BRANCH

Starting Out

- What are senators and representatives?
- Do you know the names of any senators or representatives?

Warming Up

Gaining Time

During the INS interview, you may forget how to answer a question you have studied. What can you do?

Here are some ways people respond if they forget an answer.

Practice with a Partner

What is the difference between these situations?
What will you do if you can't remember an answer?

Government

The Legislative Branch

In 1787, the United States had a problem. People argued about how the legislative branch should be.

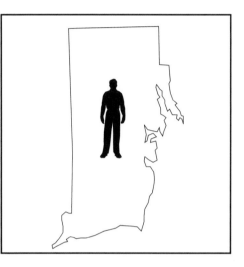

People from big states, like New York, said that each state should have a different number of representatives, depending how many people lived there. People from small states like Rhode Island did not like this idea. They wanted each state to have the same number of representatives.

The states could not agree, so they used both ideas. This is why Congress has two parts.

HOUSE OF REPRESENTATIVES

SENATE

Government

The Legislative Branch

Congress is the legislative branch of government. The members of Congress are called senators and representatives. Congress makes federal laws. Note: A bill is an idea for a law before it is signed by the president. The Congress can:

Write bills

Talk about bills

Vote on bills

SENATE
80 YES 20 NO

HOUSE
400 YES 35 NO

Send bills to the president for his or her signature

Only Congress can declare war on another country.

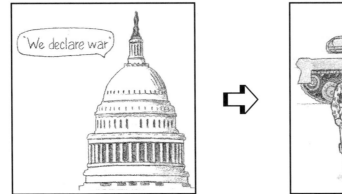

Government

The Legislative Branch

There are two (2) chambers in Congress.

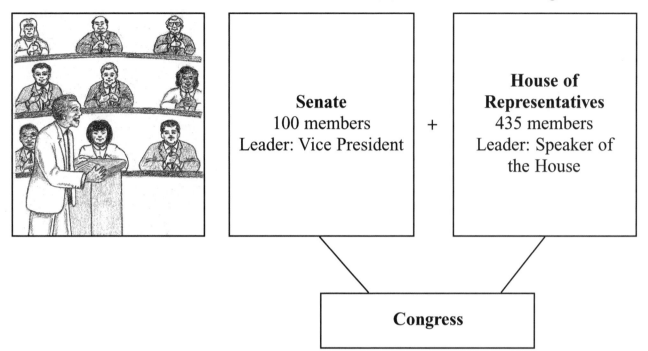

Senate
100 members
Leader: Vice President

+

House of Representatives
435 members
Leader: Speaker of the House

Congress

Congress meets in the Capitol building in Washington, D.C.

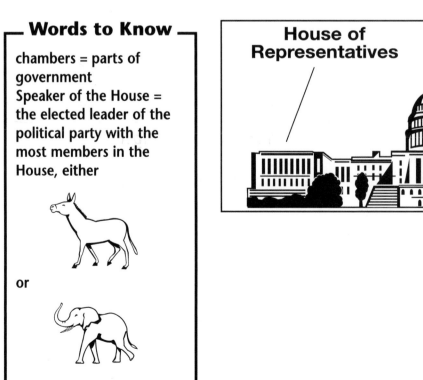

Words to Know

chambers = parts of government
Speaker of the House = the elected leader of the political party with the most members in the House, either

or

House of Representatives   Senate

Government

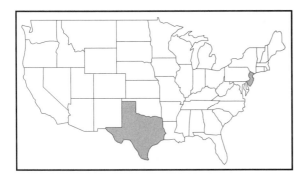

The Senate

There are two (2) senators from each state. Each of the fifty (50) states has equal power in the Senate.

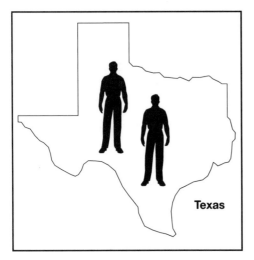

Texas

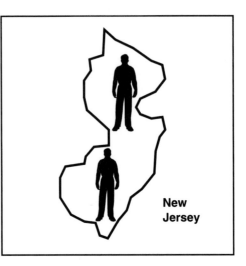

New Jersey

Practice

How many senators are there in Congress? __100__

Who are the senators from your state? ILLINOIS DICK Durbin
Peter Fitzgerald

Write the names of your senators and circle their political parties.

Senator Name	Democrat	Republican
DICK Durbin		
Peter Fitzgerald		

Government

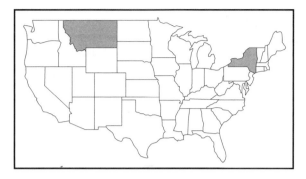

The House of Representatives

There are 435 representatives or voting members in the House of Representatives.

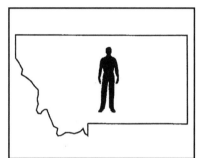

One representative in Congress

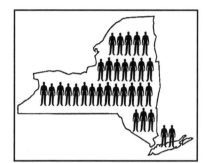

31 representatives in Congress

Words to Know

Representative district = area of land

The number of representatives depends on how many people live in a state. States with many people have more representatives. Each state is divided into districts. Each district in a state has one representative.

Practice

How many districts are there in Montana? _____One_____

How many in New York? _____31_____

How many representatives are from your state? _____

Who is your representative? Write the name of your representative and circle the political party.

Representative Name   **Democrat**   **Republican**

_____

Government

Congressional Elections

645,000 Votes   1,450,988 Votes

Words to Know

candidate
elected official

Members of the U.S. Congress—senators and representatives—are elected by the people. The candidate for senator or representative who gets the most votes wins the election. For that reason, members of Congress are called elected officials.

Practice

How many elected officials are in Congress?

100 _____Senators_____ + 435 _____representatives_____ =

Government

Congressional Terms of Office

Each time an elected official wins the vote, he or she serves a term of office. Senators and representatives can serve many terms in office. There is no limit.

1991   1993   1995   1997

This representative won the elections in these years.

How many terms has this representative been elected? _____

For how long do we elect representatives?

For _____ years.

1990   1996

This senator won the elections in these years.

How many terms has this senator been elected? _____

For how long do we elect senators?

For _____ years.

Practice

Fill in the chart.

CONGRESS

What does Congress do?

make Laws

REPRESENTATIVES

How many?
_435_

Who elects?
the people

How often elected?
2 yrs.

How many terms?
NO Limit

Leader?
Speaker of the house

SENATORS

How many?
_100_

Who elects?
the people.

How often elected?
6 yrs.

How many terms?
unlimited

Leader?
Vice President

Dictation Practice

There are many sentences in the dictation about Congress.
Complete the sentences as your teacher reads.

1. _____ Congress _____ meets in Washington, D.C.

2. There are ___ three ___ Branches ___ of government.

3. Congress ___ makes ___ laws ___ in the United States.

4. Only Congress can ___ declare ___ war ___ .

5. The ___ house ___ and ___ Senate ___ are parts of Congress.

Write the sentences as your teacher reads.

1. ___ the President is elected every four yrs. ___

2. ___ people in America have the Right to freedom ___

The Test

Circle the correct answer.   the   *Legrsxlative*

1. What branch of government is
   Congress?
   a. federal
   b. executive
   (c.) legislative
   d. judicial

2. Who makes the federal laws in
   the United States?
   (a.) Congress
   b. the Constitution
   c. the Capitol
   d. Thomas Jefferson

3. Who elects Congress?
   a. the Constitution
   (b.) the people (U.S. citizens)
   c. the Senate
   d. the House of Representatives

4. For how long do we elect each
   senator?
   a. two (2) years
   b. four (4) years
   (c.) six (6) years
   d. eight (8) years

5. For how long do we elect the
   representatives?
   (a.) two (2) years
   b. four (4) years
   c. six (6) years
   d. eight (8) years

6. How many voting members are
   in the House of Representatives?
   a. 2
   b. 100
   c. 400
   (d.) 435

7. Who is the leader of the House
   of Representatives?
   a. president
   b. vice president
   (c.) speaker of the House
   d. senator

8. Why are there 100 senators in
   the U.S. Senate?
   (a.) two from each state
   b. four from 25 states
   c. 10 x 10
   d. stars on the flag

9. How many times may a senator
   be re-elected?
   a. one time
   b. two times
   c. four times
   (d.) any number

10. How many times may a
    Congressional representative be
    re-elected?
    a. one time
    b. two times
    c. four times
    (d.) any number

11. Who has the power to declare war?
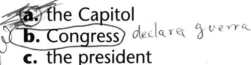
    a. the Capitol
    b. Congress declara guerra
    c. the president
    d. all of the above

12. What is the United States Capitol?
    a. the place where Congress meets
    b. the place where the president lives
    c. the place where the senators live
    d. the place where the Supreme Court meets

13. Where does Congress meet?
    a. in Washington state
    b. in the Supreme Court, in Washington, D.C.
    c. in the White House, in Washington, D.C.
    d. In the Capitol, in Washington, D.C.

14. Can you name the two U.S. senators from your state?
    1. _Peter Fitzgerald_
    _____
    2. _Dick Durbin_
    _____

15. What is Congress?
    a. the Senate and the House of Representatives
    b. the highest law of the land
    c. the first ten amendments to the Constitution
    d. the home of the president.

16. What are the duties of Congress?
    a. freedom of speech, press, and religion
    b. to elect the president
    c. to make laws
    d. to interpret the laws

Unit 10
THE EXECUTIVE BRANCH

HOME WORK

GEORGE Washington   Abraham Lincon   J.F. KENNEDY

JFK

Jeffrey KENNEDY

Starting Out

- Do you know the names of these famous presidents? Who are they?

- Who is the current president of the United States?   GEORGE W BUSH

- Who is the vice president?

  DICK cheney

Warming Up

Worries About the Test

What worries you about the INS citizenship test?

Circle yes or no, then write the number of classmates who agree.

Worries	You		Number who agree
a. I will feel bad.	Yes	No	_____
b. I will get sick.	Yes	No	_____
c. I will get nervous.	Yes	No	_____
d. I will forget everything.	Yes	No	_____
e. I will not understand.	Yes	No	_____

Practice

You can support your classmates. Write the letter of each worry next to its answer.

_____ **You are strong.**

_____ **You are good.**

_____ **You are smart.**

_____ **You can do it.**

_____ **You know a lot.**

Government

The Executive Branch

The Executive Branch enforces the laws.

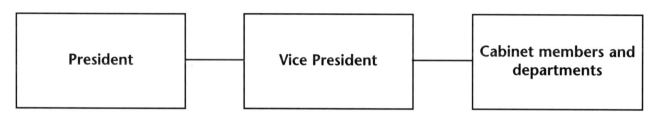

Some of the President's Responsibilities

Write the number of the responsibility in the picture.

1. Commander-in-Chief of the U.S. Military (Armed Forces)
2. Chief Executive Officer
3. Signs bills into law
4. Appoints the cabinet and members of the Supreme Court

Government

Requirements to be President

According to the Constitution, a person who wants to become president must meet certain requirements.

Write the number of the requirement in each picture.

1. Age 35 or older
2. Living in the U.S. for the past 14 years
3. Born in the U.S.
4. U.S. citizen

Practice with a Partner

Which requirements do you meet to be president of the United States? Which requirements do your children meet? Your grandchildren?

Government

The White House

The president lives and works in the White House. The address of the White House is 1600 Pennsylvania Avenue, Washington, D.C. ~~ADRESS~~

Washington, D.C., is the capital of the United States. D.C. stands for the District of Columbia. It is not a state.

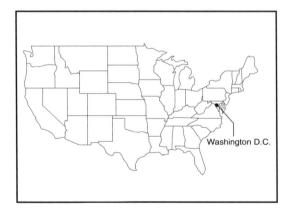

What is the capital of your native country?

MEXICO CITY

Government

Presidential Election

**Reagan
1981-89**

**Bush
1989-93**

**Clinton
1993-2001**

How often is the president elected?

Every _____ years.

A president's term of office is four years.

How many years did President Reagan serve? _____

How many terms? _____

How may years did President Bush serve? _____

How many terms? _____

Government

Presidential Election

The election for the president is in November.

I promise to uphold the Constitution.

The president is inaugurated the following January.

Words to Know

inaugurated = when the president starts the job
resigns = quits
impeached = to remove the president from his or her job

Practice

When is the next election for president?

_____

When is the next presidential inauguration? (unless the president resigns, is impeached, or dies in office)? _____

Government

Presidential Election

The people do not elect the president, the electoral college does.

In every state the candidate who has the majority of the votes gets all of the electoral votes in that state. The candidate that gets the majority of electoral votes wins the election.

Three weeks after the people vote for president, the electoral college representatives go to Washington, D.C. They vote for the candidate who won the election in their state.

Government

Presidential Succession

The president of the United States can serve only two terms.

How many years can a president serve? (see page 133) _____

(see page 133)

⌐ Words to Know ⌐

tie = equal number of votes
for and votes against.

The vice president is elected with the president. The vice president leads the Senate. He or she only votes if there is a tie on a Senate vote.

If the president dies, resigns or is impeached while in office. . .

If the president and vice president die while in office. . .

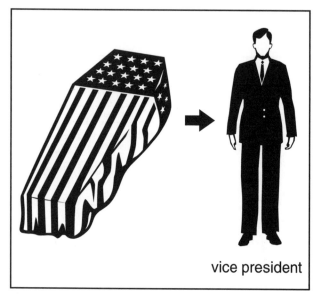

vice president

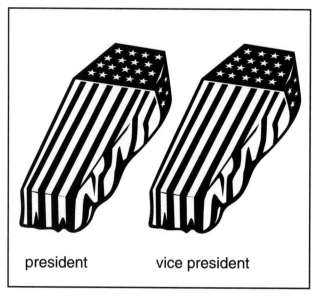

president   vice president

the vice president becomes president.

the speaker of the house becomes president.

Practice with a Partner

If the president died today, who would become president?

_____ Sp VICE PRESIDENT _____

If the president and the vice president died today, who would become

president? SpEACKER of the House _____

Government

The Cabinet

The cabinet is a special group of people who advise the president. Each cabinet member is the leader of a department of government.

The president appoints the Cabinet.

president

Defense

Education

Housing

Labor

Health and Human Services

Agriculture

State

Treasury

Transportation

INS

Justice

Veteran Affairs

Commerce

Interior

Energy

Government

Practice with a Partner

Make a question and then answer it.

Where?

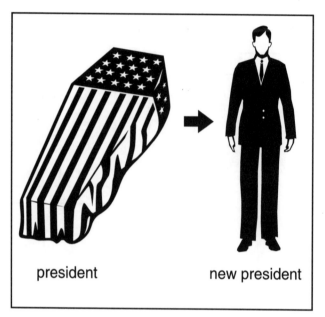

president   new president

Who?

Presidental Election

When?

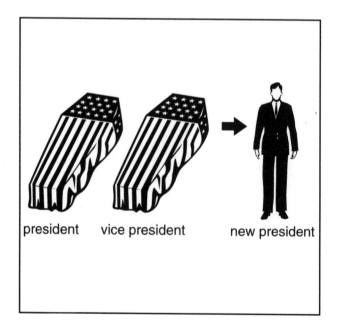

president   vice president   new president

Who?

Dictation Practice

Listen to your teacher read the sentences. Unscramble the words to make complete sentences. Write the sentences on the lines. Count the words to make sure you have them all.

1. The   Washington, D.C.   in   lives   President

The president lives in Washington, D.c.

2. president   in   the   House   The   White   lives

The president lives in the white house.

3. capital   the   Washington, D.C.   is   of   United States   The

The city of Cincinnati State is Washington D.c.

4. enforces   president   the   laws   The

The President enforces the laws.

Write the sentences as your teacher reads.

1. _____

2. _____

The Test

Circle the correct answer.

1. Who elects the president of the United States?
   a. the people
   b. Congress
   c. the electoral college
   d. the White House

2. For how long do we elect the president?
   a. two years
   b. four years
   c. six years
   d. eight years

3. Who becomes the president if the president should die?
   a. the vice president
   b. the speaker of the House
   c. Congress
   d. the oldest member of Congress

4. Who becomes president if the president and the vice president should die?
   a. the vice president
   b. the speaker of the House
   c. Congress
   d. the oldest member of Congress

5. How many full terms can a president serve?
   a. two
   b. four
   c. six
   d. eight

6. What is the White House?
   a. the president's official home
   b. where Congress meets
   c. a house on Main Street
   d. a courthouse

7. Where is the White House located?
   a. in the Capitol building
   b. Washington state
   c. in the Senate
   d. Washington, D.C. (1600 Pennsylvania Ave.)

8. What is the name of the president's official home?
   a. the White House
   b. Congress
   c. the Capitol
   d. Washington, D.C.

9. Who is the Commander-in-Chief of the U.S. military?
   a. the top general
   b. the speaker of the House
   c. the president
   d. the vice president

10. In what month do we vote for the president?
    a. January
    b. March
    c. September
    d. November

11. In which month is the new president inaugurated?
    a. January *(circled)*
    b. March
    c. September
    d. November

12. Name a requirement to be president.
    a. be 35 years old
    b. born in the U.S. *(circled)*
    c. living in the U.S. last 14 years
    d. all of the above

13. What is the executive branch of our government?
    a. Congress
    b. the president, vice president, cabinet *(circled)*
    c. Capitol
    d. executive, legislative, judicial

14. Who signs bills into laws?
    a. senators
    b. representatives
    c. president *(circled)*
    d. vice president

15. What special group advises the president?
    a. the cabinet *(circled)*
    b. Congress
    c. the Supreme Court
    d. the Bill of Rights

16. Who is the president of the United States today? What is his full name?
    GEORGE W BUSH

17. Who is the vice president of the United States today?
    DICR CHAINEY

Unit 11
THE JUDICIAL BRANCH

Starting Out

- Who is the judge? What does she do?
- Who is the lawyer? What does he do?
- Who is on the jury? What do they do?

Warming Up

Spelling

Sometimes when people speak English they combine words. It can be difficult to hear how many words are being said. You have to listen carefully. Now listen to your teacher read a sentence.

How many words do you hear? _____

Now write the sentence.

_____

**You will need to memorize how to spell certain words.
How can you practice your spelling?**

Use picture flash cards.

Make a tape.

What else can you do to practice your spelling?

Warming Up

Word Families

Many words that look similar also have a similar meaning. They are from the same "word family."

1. The **colonists** are people who live in **colonies.**

2. **Representatives** are elected officials. They **represent** the people in their district in Congress.

3. The person who wins the **presidential** election becomes the **president.**

4. During World War II, **England** was an ally of the U.S. The **English** army fought with the allies.

5. The **judicial** branch of government is also called the **judiciary.**

Practice

Make a new word from the same family by adding (+) or subtracting (-) the letters in the parentheses ( ) and then adding *al.*

                                        + al

1. president (+ i) _____

2. Constitution   _____

3. colony (- y, + i) _____

4. Congress (+ ion) _____

5. Judiciary (- ary) _____

Government

The Judicial Branch

The judicial branch of the government explains the law.

a ceptada

The judiciary also decides if a law is allowed, according to the Constitution.

Government

The Judicial Branch

The judicial branch is made up of courts. There are local, state and federal courts. Note: interpret = explain.

Local courts

interpret

local laws.

State courts

interpret

state laws.

Federal courts

interpret

federal laws.

The Supreme Court

interprets

the Constitution.

Do you have judges in your native country?
How are they the same or different?

Government

The Judicial Branch

In most cases, the accused has the right to a trial by jury.

Words to Know

accused = the person on trial who may have broken the law

sentence = the punishment for the crime. It can be to pay money, to go to jail, or to help people in the community

In a trial by jury one lawyer tries to show the jury that the accused is guilty. The other lawyer tries to show the jury that the accused is not guilty.

The judge explains the law to the jury. The jury decides if the accused is guilty or not guilty of breaking the law. If the jury finds the accused guilty, the judge gives the sentence.

Government

The Supreme Court

The Supreme Court is the highest court in the United States. There are nine justices, or judges, on the Supreme Court. They use the Constitution and other laws of the United States to decide cases.

President

Supreme Court

Words to Know

appoints = names
justices = judges
ratifies = approves

The president appoints the justices. Congress ratifies each one. Justices serve on the Supreme Court for life.

The Supreme Court

The first woman to be a Supreme Court Justice was Sandra Day O' Connor. She was appointed by President Reagan in 1981.

Do you know the names of any other Supreme Court Justices?

Practice

Who is the Chief Justice now?

William Rehnquist

Government

The Supreme Court

At least five of the nine justices on the Supreme Court must agree to decide a case. Decisions by the Supreme Court are final.

The case is decided. Mr. M. wins.

Practice with a Partner

Does your native country have a Supreme Court?
Who makes the final decisions about laws in your native country?

Words to Know

unconstitutional = breaks the law of the Constitution

Miranda Rights

Important Supreme Court Decision

Miranda versus Arizona was a very important Supreme Court case. Ernesto Miranda was arrested. The police asked Mr. Miranda many questions. He answered the questions and signed a paper that said, "I am guilty." He did not have a lawyer with him to help answer the questions. In court, the jury found Miranda guilty. He was sent to prison.

Miranda brought his case to the Supreme Court. He believed the police should have told him he could have a lawyer before they asked questions. The Supreme Court agreed with Mr. Miranda.

Now all police officers must read these Miranda Rights to people arrested for a crime.

1. You have the right to remain silent.

2. Anything you say can and will be used against you in court.

3. You have the right to talk to a lawyer before you answer questions.

4. You have the right to have a lawyer with you while you answer questions.

5. If you cannot afford a lawyer, you have the right to one for free in most criminal cases.

What will you do if you are arrested?

Practice

Write the branch of government under the picture.

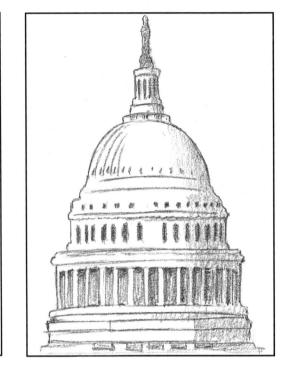

Judicial   Executive   Legislative

Practice

Fill in the chart with the correct information.

Branch	Legislative	Executive	Judicial
What do they do?			
Who is the leader?			
How many members?			
How many terms?			

Dictation Practice

Listen to your teacher read the sentences. Unscramble the words to make complete sentences. Write the sentences on the lines. Count the words to make sure you have them all.

1. citizens   the   United   All   have   vote   right   to   States

   ✗ All Citizensofthe United states have right to vote.
   ✓ All United States citizens have the right to vote.

2. home   America   the   the   is   brave   of

   America is the. home of the. brave

3. citizen   must   The   be   president   American   an

   the president must be an the American Citizen

4. have   People   freedom   to   the   America   right   in

   People in America have theright to freedom

5. Washington, DC   the   is   United   capital   States   of

   washington, DC. is the Capital of United states

Write the sentences as your teacher reads.

1. _____

2. _____

The Test

Circle the correct answer.

1. What is the judicial branch of our government?
   a. Congress
   b. the Cabinet
   c. the Supreme Court
   d. none of the above

2. What are the duties of the Supreme Court?
   a. make laws
   b. enforce laws
   c. interpret laws
   d. all of the above

3. Who is the Chief Justice of the Supreme Court?
   a. William Clinton
   b. Ronald Reagan
   c. William Rehnquist
   d. George Bush

4. What is the highest court in the United States?
   a. local court
   b. state court
   c. federal court
   d. Supreme Court

5. How many Supreme Court justices are there?
   a. one
   b. three
   c. six
   d. nine

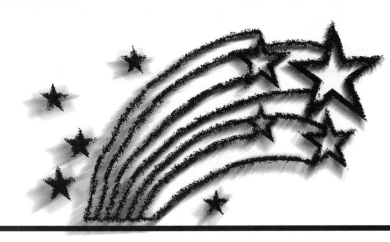

Unit 12
STATE AND LOCAL GOVERNMENT

New York

California

State

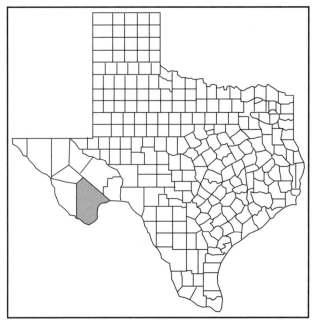

County

City

GENERAL STORE

Offices

SALE SALE SALE

SALE

Police

Town or Village

Starting Out

- What is the name of your state? your county?

- Do you live in a city, town, or village?

Warming Up

Confidence at the Interview

You want to feel confident until the end of your interview. What may help you?

Think positive thoughts. What words make you feel confident?

I am good.   I know a lot.   _____

I am smart.   I can do it.   _____

Sit confidently. How will you sit?

_____

Speak confidently. How will you speak?

_____

Think about each part of the interview.

Imagine

Pray

Practice in front of a mirror

Practice with a Partner

What will you do to help you feel confident at the INS interview?

Government

State Government

Most state governments have three branches:

Executive

Governor
Lieutenant Governor
State Agencies

Legislative

State Senators
State Representatives

Judicial

State Supreme Court
Lower State Courts

Government

State Capitals

State governments are located in the state capital.

What is the name of your state?

ILLINOIS

What is the name of your state capital?

SPRINGFIELD

State Government

The Executive Branch

A governor is the head executive of state government or the state's chief executive officer. The lieutenant governor assists the governor. The governor has many responsibilities.

signs state bills into state laws

leader of the State National Guard

Practice

Who is your governor? Write the name of your governor and circle the political party.

Governor Name	Democrat	Republican
GEORGE RYAN		

The executive branch of state government also manages many state agencies.

state lottery

state highways

driver's license

State Government

The Legislative Branch

The State Legislature usually has a Senate and a House of Representatives. State senators and representatives are elected by the people. One senator is elected from each state senate district. One representative is elected from each assembly district.

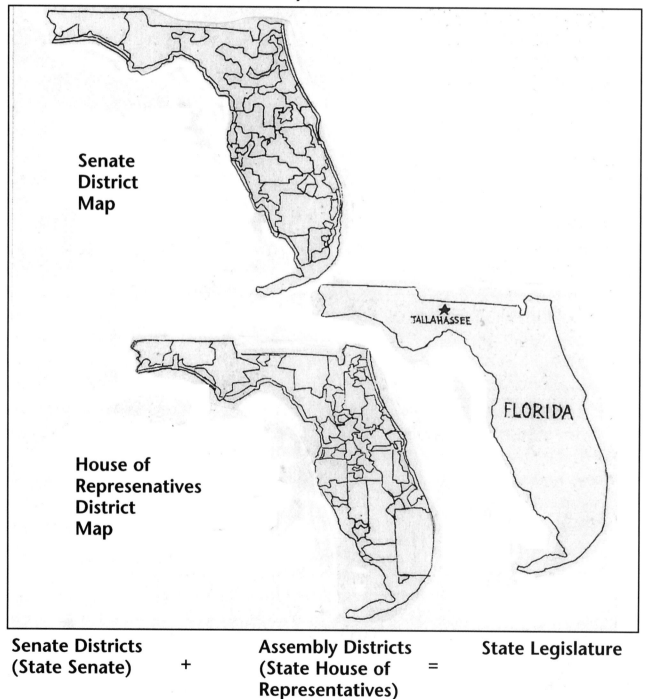

Senate
District
Map

House of
Represenatives
District
Map

| Senate Districts (State Senate) | + | Assembly Districts (State House of Representatives) | = | State Legislature |

State Government: The Legislative Branch

Practice

1. Who is your State Senator? Write the name of your state senator and circle the political party.

State Senator Name	Democrat	Republican
DICK DURBIN PETER FINGERALD		

2. Who is your State Representative? Write the name of your state representative or assembly person and circle the political party.

State Representative Name	Democrat	Republican

State senators and State representatives have many responsibilities.

Drunk Driving: The Legal Limit in this State is an Alcohol Content of...

make state laws

State Income Tax Return Form -1040

Step 1

Step 2

Step 3

decide how much money to charge for state taxes

State Government

Judicial Branch

The state courts interpret state laws. The courts must follow the state constitution, the federal courts, and the U.S. Constitution and Bill of Rights.

criminal court

civil court

County Government

County government is the largest local government. It is directed by a board of supervisors or commissioners. They are the executive and legislative branch together.

County government has many responsibilities.

jails

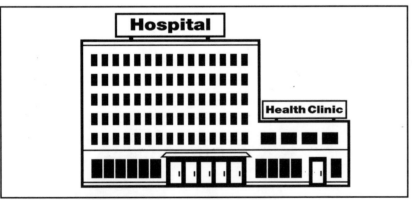

public health clinics and hospitals

What is the name of your county?

_____

Local Government

City, Town and Village

An elected mayor is usually the head executive of city, town, or village government. The mayor heads the executive branch of government.

The legislative branch is often a city council with elected representatives.

Sometimes there is no mayor or city council. Instead, there is a city manager or an elected city commission.

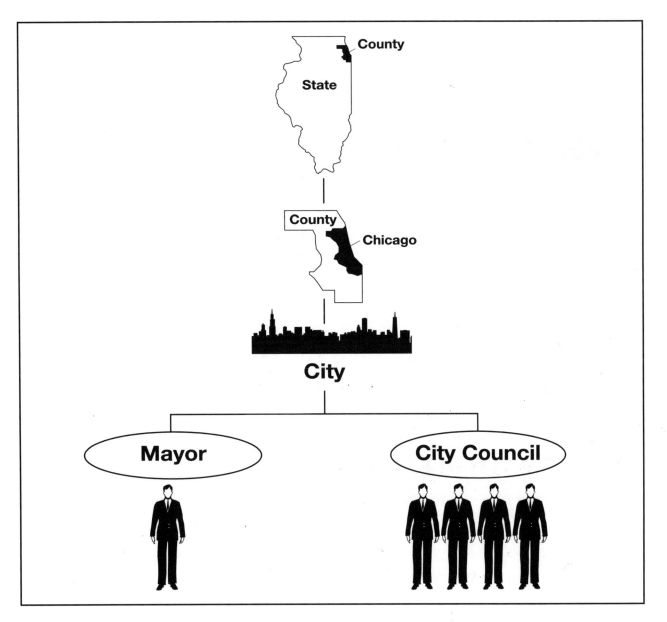

Responsibilities of Local Government

libraries

garbage collection

fire department

public transportation

parks

law enforcement

Practice with a Partner

Who is the head of your city, town, or village? What is his or her title?

Is there a city council where you live? What is it called?

Practice

Fill in the flow charts.

State   County   Local   Governor   Mayor

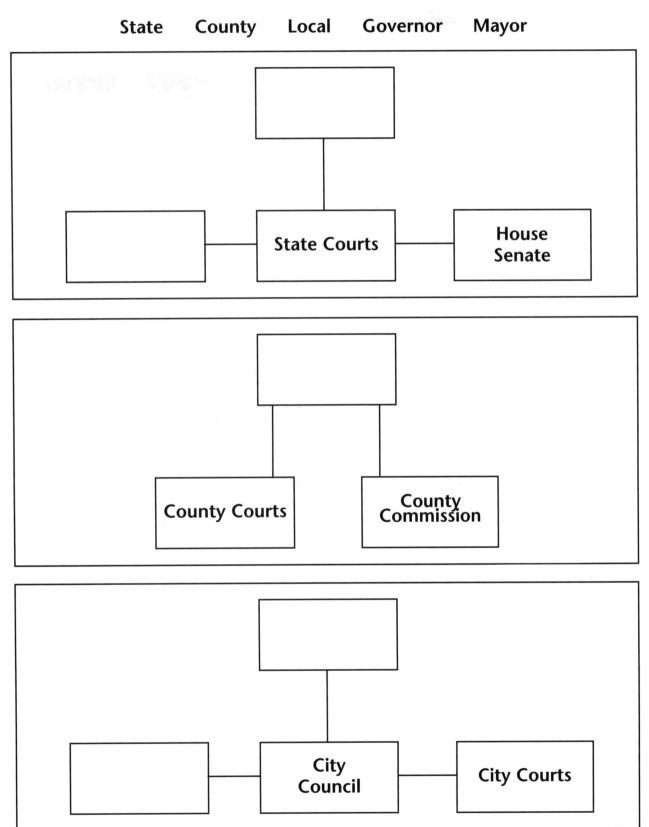

Dictation Practice

Write five sentences using a phrase from each column.

A	B	C
The people	3	states in the Union.
The president	in the class	from France.
The Statue of Liberty	50	took a citizenship test.
There are	must be born	branches of government.
There are	was a gift	in the United States.

1. The people in the class took a citizenship test

2. The president must be born in the United State

3. The Statue of Liberty was a gift from france

4. There are 50 states in the Union

5. There are 3 branches of government.

Write the sentences as your teacher reads.

1. _____

2. _____

The Test

Circle or write the correct answer.

1. What is the head executive of city government called?
   a. governor
   b. senator
   c. mayor *(circled)*
   d. representative

2. What is the name of the head executive of state government?
   a. governor *(circled)*
   b. senator
   c. mayor
   d. representative

3. Who is the head of your local government?

   MIKE FORTNER

4. What is the capital of your state?

   ILLINOIS

5. Who is the current governor of your state?

   GEORGE Ryan

Sample N-400 Form

Print clearly or type your answers using **CAPITAL** letters. Failure to print clearly may delay your application. Use blue or black ink.

Part 1. Your Name *(The Person Applying for Naturalization)*

Write your INS "A"- number here:
A 35490 10 34

A. Your current legal name.

Family Name *(Last Name)*
Garcia D

Given Name *(First Name)*
DELIA

Full Middle Name *(if applicable)*

FOR INS USE ONLY

Bar Code	Date Stamp

B. Your name <u>exactly</u> as it appears on your Permanent Resident Card.

Family Name *(Last Name)*
GARCIA

Given Name *(First Name)*
DELIA

Full Middle Name *(if applicable)*

C. If you have ever used other names, provide them below.

Family Name *(Last Name)*	Given Name *(First Name)*	Middle Name
DELIA		
Hernandez	DELIA	

Remarks

D. Name change *(optional)*

Please read the Instructions before you decide whether to change your name.

1. Would you like to legally change your name? ☐ Yes ☒ No

2. If "Yes," print the new name you would like to use. Do not use initials or abbreviations when writing your new name.

Family Name *(Last Name)*

Given Name *(First Name)*

Full Middle Name

Action

Part 2. Information About Your Eligibility *(Check Only One.)*

I am at least 18 years old **AND**

A. ☒ I have been a Lawful Permanent Resident of the United States for at least 5 years.

B. ☐ I have been a Lawful Permanent Resident of the United States for at least 3 years, AND
I have been married to and living with the same U.S. citizen for the last 3 years, AND
my spouse has been a U.S. citizen for the last 3 years.

C. ☐ I am applying on the basis of qualifying military service.

D. ☐ Other (please explain) _____

_____

Sample N-400 Form

<table>
<tr><td>

Part 3. Information About You

</td><td>

Write your INS "A"- number here:

A 3 5 4 9 6 1 0 3 4

</td></tr>
</table>

A. Social Security Number

354-96-1034

B. Date of Birth *(Month/Day/Year)*

09/20/1967

C. Date You Became a Permanent Resident *(Month/Day/Year)*

02/07/199_

D. Country of Birth

Mexico

E. Country of Nationality

Mexicana

F. Are either of your parents U.S. citizens? *(if yes, see Instructions)* ☐ Yes ☒ No

G. What is your current marital status? ☐ Single, Never Married ☒ Married ☐ Divorced ☐ Widowed

☐ Marriage Annulled or Other (explain) _____

H. Did you attach a Form N-648 because of a disability or impairment that prevents you from passing the tests of English and/or U.S. History and Government? ☐ Yes ☐ No

I. Are you requesting an accommodation to the naturalization process because of a disability or impairment? (See Instructions for some examples of accommodations.) ☐ Yes ☐ No

If you answered "Yes," check the box below that applies:

☐ I am deaf or hearing impaired and need a sign language interpreter who uses the following language: _____

☐ I use a wheelchair.

☐ I am blind or sight impaired.

☐ I will need another type of accommodation. Please explain: _____

_____

_____

Part 4. Addresses and Telephone Numbers

A. Home Address - Street Number and Name *(do NOT write a P.O. Box in this space)*

307. E. FOREST Ave.

Apartment Number

City	County	State	ZIP Code
West Chicago		Illinois	60185

B. Mailing Address - Street Number and Name *(if different from home address)*

Apartment Number

City	State	ZIP Code	Country

C. Daytime Phone Number *(if any)*

(630) 8768136

Evening Phone Number *(if any)*

(630) 5625961

E-mail Address *(if any)*

Form N2400 (Rev 2/11/2000)N

Sample N-400 Form

Part 5. Information for Criminal Records Search

Note: The categories below are those required by the FBI. See Instructions for more information.

A. Gender

☐ Male ☒ Female

B. Height

5 Feet 4 Inches

C. Weight

170 Pounds

D. Race

☐ White ☐ Asian or Pacific Islander ☐ Black ☐ Native American or Alaskan Native ☐ Other

E. Hair color

☐ Black ☑ Brown ☐ Blonde ☐ Gray ☐ White ☐ Red ☐ Sandy ☐ Bald (No Hair)

F. Eye color

☑ Brown ☐ Blue ☐ Green ☐ Hazel ☐ Gray ☐ Black ☐ Pink ☐ Maroon ☐ Other

Part 6. Information About Your Residence and Employment

A. Where have you lived during the last 5 years? Begin with where you live now and then list every place you lived for the last 5 years. If you need more space, use a separate sheet of paper.

Street Number and Name, Apartment Number, City, State, Zip Code and Country	Dates (Month/Year)	
	From	To
Current Home Address	_ _ / _ _ _ _	Present
	_ _ / _ _ _ _	_ _ / _ _ _ _
	_ _ / _ _ _ _	_ _ / _ _ _ _
	_ _ / _ _ _ _	_ _ / _ _ _ _
	_ _ / _ _ _ _	_ _ / _ _ _ _

B. Where have you worked (or, if you were a student, what schools did you attend) during the last 5 years? Include military service. Begin with your current or latest employer and then list every place you have worked or studied for the last 5 years. If you need more space, use a separate sheet of paper.

Employer or School Name	Employer or School Address (Street,City and State)	Dates (Month/Year)		Your Occupation
		From	To	
		_ _ / _ _ _ _	_ _ / _ _ _ _	
		_ _ / _ _ _ _	_ _ / _ _ _ _	
		_ _ / _ _ _ _	_ _ / _ _ _ _	
		_ _ / _ _ _ _	_ _ / _ _ _ _	
		_ _ / _ _ _ _	_ _ / _ _ _ _	

Sample N-400 Form

Part 7. Time Outside the United States	Write your INS "A"- number here:
(Including Trips to Canada, Mexico, and the Caribbean Islands)	A _ _ _ _ _ _ _ _ _

A. How many total days did you spend outside of the United States during the past 5 years (Count days on all trips that last 24 hours or more).   [____] days

B. How many trips of 24 hours or more have you taken outside of the United States during the past 5 years?   [____] trips

C. List below all the trips of 24 hours or more that you have taken outside of the United States since becoming a Lawful Permanent Resident. Begin with your most recent trip. If you need more space, use a separate sheet of paper.

Date You Left the United States *(Month/Day/Year)*	Date You Returned to the United States *(Month/Day/Year)*	Did Trip Last 6 Months or More?	Countries to Which You Traveled	Total Days Out of the United States
_ _ / _ _ / _ _ _ _	_ _ / _ _ / _ _ _ _	☐ Yes ☐ No		
_ _ / _ _ / _ _ _ _	_ _ / _ _ / _ _ _ _	☐ Yes ☐ No		
_ _ / _ _ / _ _ _ _	_ _ / _ _ / _ _ _ _	☐ Yes ☐ No		
_ _ / _ _ / _ _ _ _	_ _ / _ _ / _ _ _ _	☐ Yes ☐ No		
_ _ / _ _ / _ _ _ _	_ _ / _ _ / _ _ _ _	☐ Yes ☐ No		
_ _ / _ _ / _ _ _ _	_ _ / _ _ / _ _ _ _	☐ Yes ☐ No		
_ _ / _ _ / _ _ _ _	_ _ / _ _ / _ _ _ _	☐ Yes ☐ No		
_ _ / _ _ / _ _ _ _	_ _ / _ _ / _ _ _ _	☐ Yes ☐ No		
_ _ / _ _ / _ _ _ _	_ _ / _ _ / _ _ _ _	☐ Yes ☐ No		
_ _ / _ _ / _ _ _ _	_ _ / _ _ / _ _ _ _	☐ Yes ☐ No		

Part 8. Information About Your Marital History

A. How many times have you been married (including annulled marriages)? [____] If you have NEVER been married, go to Part 9.

B. If you are now married, give the following information about your spouse:

1. Spouse's Family Name *(Last Name)*   GARCIA   Given Name *(First Name)*   Felipe   Full Middle Name *(if applicable)*   Felipe Jesus Garcia

2. Date of Birth *(Month/Day/Year)*   02/05/1968   3. Date of Marriage *(Month/Day/Year)*   03/__/1995   4. Spouse's Social Security Number   _ _ _ - _ _ - _ _ _ _

5. Home Address - Street Number and Name   307 E TORES Ave.   Apartment Number [____]

City   WEST CHICAGO   State   ILLINOIS   ZIP Code   60185

Sample N-400 Form

Part 8. Information About Your Marital History *(Continued)*	Write your INS "A"- number here:
	A __ __ __ __ __ __ __ __ __

C. Is your spouse a U.S. citizen? ☒ Yes   ☐ No

D. If your spouse is a U.S. citizen, give the following information:

   1. When did your spouse become a U.S. citizen? ☐ At Birth ☒ Other

     If "Other," give the following information:

   2. Date your spouse became a U.S. citizen

     __ __ / __ __ / __ __ __ __

   3. Place your spouse became a U.S. citizen *(please see Instructions)*

                    City and State

E. If your spouse is NOT a U.S. citizen, give the following information :

   1. Spouse's Country of Citizenship

   2. Spouse's INS "A"- Number *(If applicable)*

     A __ __ __ __ __ __ __ __ __

   3. Spouse's Immigration Status

     ☐ Lawful Permanent Resident   ☐ Other _____

F. If you were married before, provide the following information about your prior spouse. If you have more than one previous marriage, use a separate sheet of paper to provide the information in questions 1-5 below.

   1. Prior Spouse's Family Name *(Last Name)*   Given Name *(First Name)*   Full Middle Name *(if applicable)*

   2. Prior Spouse's Immigration Status

     ☐ U.S. Citizen

     ☐ Lawful Permanent Resident

     ☐ Other _____

   3. Date of Marriage *(Month/Day/Year)*

     __ __ / __ __ / __ __ __ __

   4. Date Marriage Ended *(Month/Day/Year)*

     __ __ / __ __ / __ __ __ __

   5. How Marriage Ended

     ☐ Divorce ☐ Spouse Died ☐ Other _____

G. How many times has your current spouse been married (including annulled marriages)? [   ]

   If your spouse has EVER been married before, give the following information about your spouse's prior marriage.
   If your spouse has more than one previous marriage, use a separate sheet of paper to provide the information in questions 1-5 below.

   1. Prior Spouse's Family Name *(Last Name)*   Given Name *(First Name)*   Full Middle Name *(if applicable)*

   2. Prior Spouse's Immigration Status

     ☐ U.S. Citizen

     ☐ Lawful Permanent Resident

     ☐ Other _____

   3. Date of Marriage *(Month/Day/Year)*

     __ __ / __ __ / __ __ __ __

   4. Date Marriage Ended *(Month/Day/Year)*

     __ __ / __ __ / __ __ __ __

   5. How Marriage Ended

     ☐ Divorce ☐ Spouse Died ☐ Other _____

Form N5400 (Rev 2/11/2000)N

Sample N-400 Form

<table>
<tr>
<td>Part 9. Information About Your Children</td>
<td>Write your INS "A"- number here:
A _ _ _ _ _ _ _ _ _</td>
</tr>
</table>

A. How many sons and daughters have you had? For more information on which sons and daughters you should include and how to complete this section, see the Instructions. `| |`

B. Provide the following information about all of your sons and daughters. If you need more space, use a separate sheet of paper.

Full Name of Son or Daughter	Date of Birth (Month/Day/Year)	INS "A"- number (if child has one)	Country of Birth	Current Address (Street, City, State & Country)
ERIK GARCIA	09/05/1996	A _ _ _ _ _ _ _ _	Winweld IA	307 E. Fores t poe. chic w.
	_ _ / _ _ / _ _ _ _	A _ _ _ _ _ _ _ _		
	_ _ / _ _ / _ _ _ _	A _ _ _ _ _ _ _ _		
	_ _ / _ _ / _ _ _ _	A _ _ _ _ _ _ _ _		
	_ _ / _ _ / _ _ _ _	A _ _ _ _ _ _ _ _		
	_ _ / _ _ / _ _ _ _	A _ _ _ _ _ _ _ _		
	_ _ / _ _ / _ _ _ _	A _ _ _ _ _ _ _ _		
	_ _ / _ _ / _ _ _ _	A _ _ _ _ _ _ _ _		

Part 10. Additional Questions

Please answer questions 1 through 14. If you answer "Yes" to any of these questions, include a written explanation with this form. Your written explanation should (1) explain why your answer was "Yes," and (2) provide any additional information that helps to explain your answer.

A. General Questions

1. Have you **EVER** claimed to be a U.S. citizen *(in writing or any other way)?* ☐ Yes ☒ No
2. Have you **EVER** registered to vote in any federal, state, or local election in the United States? ☐ Yes ☒ No
3. Have you **EVER** voted in any federal, state, or local election in the United States? ☐ Yes ☒ No
4. Since becoming a lawful Permanent Resident, have you **EVER** failed to file a required federal, state, or local tax return? ☐ Yes ☒ No
5. Do you owe any federal, state, or local taxes that are overdue? ☐ Yes ☒ No
6. Do you have any title of nobility in any foreign country? ☐ Yes ☒ No
7. Have you ever been declared legally incompetent or been confined to a mental institution? ☐ Yes ☐ No

Form N-400 (Rev. 02/11/2000)N

Sample N-400 Form

Write your INS "A"- number here:

A _ _ _ _ _ _ _ _

B. Affiliations

8. a. Have you **EVER** been a member of or associated with any organization, association, fund, foundation, party, club, society, or similar group in the United States or in any other place? ☐ Yes ☒ No

     b. If you answered "Yes," list the name of each group below. If you need more space, attach the names of the other group(s) on a separate sheet of paper.

Name of Group	Name of Group
1.	6.
2.	7.
3.	8.
4.	9.
5.	10.

9. Have you **EVER** been a member of or in any way associated *(either directly or indirectly)* with:

    a. The Communist Party? ☐ Yes ☒ No

    b. Any other totalitarian party? ☐ Yes ☒ No

    c. A terrorist organization? ☐ Yes ☒ No

10. Have you **EVER** advocated *(either directly or indirectly)* the overthrow of any government by force or violence? ☐ Yes ☒ No

11. Have you **EVER** persecuted *(either directly or indirectly)* any person because of race, religion, national origin, membership in a particular social group, or political opinion? ☐ Yes ☒ No

12. Between March 23, 1933, and May 8, 1945, did you work for or associate in any way *(either directly or indirectly)* with:

    a. The Nazi government of Germany? ☐ Yes ☒ No

    b. Any government in any area (1) occupied by, (2) allied with, or (3) established with the help of the Nazi government of Germany? ☐ Yes ☒ No

    c. Any German, Nazi, or S.S. military unit, paramilitary unit, self-defense unit, vigilante unit citizen unit, extermination camp, concentration camp, prisoner of war camp, prison, labor camp, or transit camp? ☐ Yes ☒ No

C. Continuous Residence

Since becoming a Lawful Permanent Resident of the United States:

13. Have you **EVER** called yourself a "nonresident" on a federal, state, or local tax return? ☐ Yes ☐ No

14. Have you **EVER** failed to file a federal, state, or local tax return because you considered yourself to be a "nonresident"? ☐ Yes ☐ No

Form N-400 (Rev. 2/1120/00)N

Sample N-400 Form

A _ _ _ _ _ _ _ _

D. Good Moral Character

For the purposes of this application, you must answer "Yes" to the following questions even if your records were sealed, expunged, or otherwise cleared or if anyone, including a judge, law enforcement officer, or attorney, told you that you no longer have a record.

15. Have you **EVER** been arrested, cited, or detained by any law enforcement officer (including INS and military officers) for any reason? ☐ Yes ☒ No

16. Have you **EVER** committed a crime or offense for which you were NOT arrested? ☐ Yes ☒ No

17. Have you **EVER** been charged with committing any crime or offense? ☐ Yes ☒ No

18. Have you **EVER** been convicted of a crime or offense? ☐ Yes ☒ No

19. Have you **EVER** been placed in an alternative sentencing or a rehabilitative program (for example: diversion, deferred prosecution, withheld adjudication, deferred adjudication?) ☐ Yes ☒ No

20. Have you **EVER** received a suspended sentence, been placed on probation, or been paroled? ☐ Yes ☒ No

21. Have you **EVER** been in jail or prison? ☐ Yes ☒ No

If you answered "Yes" to any of questions 15 through 21, complete the following table. If you need more space, use a separate sheet of paper to give the same information.

Why were you arrested, cited, detained, or charged?	Date arrested, cited, detained, or charged *(Month/Day/Year)*	Where were you arrested, cited, detained or charged? *(City, State, Country)*	Outcome or disposition of the arrest, citation, detention or charge *(no charges filed, charges dismissed, jail, probation, etc.)*

Answer questions 22 through 33. If you answer "Yes" to any of these questions, include a written explanation with this form. Your written explanation should (1) explain why your answer was "Yes," and (2) provide any additional information that helps explain your answer.

22. Have you **EVER:**

   a. been a habitual drunkard? ☐ Yes ☒ No

   b. been a prostitute, or procured anyone for prostitution? ☐ Yes ☒ No

   c. sold or smuggled controlled substances, illegal drugs or narcotics? ☐ Yes ☒ No

   d. been married to more than one person at the same time? ☐ Yes ☒ No

   e. helped anyone enter or try to enter the United States illegally? ☐ Yes ☒ No

   f. gambled illegally or received income from illegal gambling? ☐ Yes ☒ No

   g. failed to support your dependents or to pay alimony? ☐ Yes ☒ No

23. Have you **EVER** given false or misleading information to any U.S. government official while applying for any immigration benefit or to prevent deportation, exclusion, or removal? ☐ Yes ☒ No

24. Have you **EVER** lied to any U.S. government official to gain entry or admission into the United States? ☐ Yes ☒ No

Sample N-400 Form

Part 10. Additional Questions *(Continued)*	Write your INS "A"- number here:
	A _ _ _ _ _ _ _ _ _

E. Removal, Exclusion, and Deportation Proceedings

25. Are removal, exclusion, rescission or deportation proceedings pending against you? ☐ Yes ☒ No

26. Have you **EVER** been removed, excluded, or deported from the United States? ☐ Yes ☒ No

27. Have you **EVER** been ordered to be removed, excluded, or deported from the United States? ☐ Yes ☒ No

28. Have you **EVER** applied for any kind of relief from removal, exclusion, or deportation? ☐ Yes ☒ No

F. Military Service

29. Have you **EVER** served in the U.S. Armed Forces? ☒ Yes ☒ No

30. Have you **EVER** left the United States to avoid being drafted into the U.S. Armed Forces? ☐ Yes ☒ No

31. Have you **EVER** applied for any kind of exemption from military service in the U.S. Armed Forces? ☒ Yes ☒ No

32. Have you **EVER** deserted from the U.S. Armed Forces? ☐ Yes ☒ No

G. Selective Service Registration

33. Are you a male who lived in the United States at any time between your 18th and 26th birthdays in any status except as a lawful nonimmigrant? ☐ Yes ☒ No

   If NO, go to question 34.

   If YES, provide the information below. If you have NOT YET REGISTERED and are still <u>under the age of 26</u>, you must register before you apply for naturalization, so that you can complete the information below:

Date Registered (Month/Day/Year)	[ ]	Selective Service Number	_ _ / _ _ / _ _ _ _
Classification	[ ]	Local Board Number	[ ]

   If YES, but you did NOT register with the Selective Service and you are now <u>26 years old or older</u>, attach a statement explaining why you did not register.

H. Oath Requirements *(See Part 14 for the full text of the Oath)*

Answer questions 34 through 39. If you answer "No" to any of these questions, include a written explanation with this form. Your written explanation should (1) explain why your answer was "No" and (2) provide any additional information that helps explain your answer.

34. Do you support the Constitution and form of government of the United States? ☒ Yes ☐ No

35. Do you understand the full Oath of Allegiance to the United States? ☒ Yes ☐ No

36. Are you willing to take the full Oath of Allegiance to the United States? ☒ Yes ☐ No

37. If the law requires it, are you willing to bear arms on behalf of the United States? ☒ Yes ☐ No

38. If the law requires it, are you willing to perform noncombatant services in the U.S. Armed Forces? ☒ Yes ☐ No

39. If the law requires it, are you willing to perform work of national importance under civilian direction? ☐ Yes ☐ No

Form N-400 (Rev.2/11/2000)N

Sample N-400 Form

Part 11. Your Signature	Write your INS "A"- number here:
	A — — — — — — — — —

I certify, under penalty of perjury under the laws of the United States of America, that this application, and the evidence submitted with it, are all true and correct. I also authorize the release of any information which INS needs to determine my eligibility for naturalization.

Your Signature

Date *(Month/Day/Year)*

__ __ / __ __ / __ __ __ __

Part 12. Signature of Person Who Prepared This Application for You *(if applicable)*

I declare under penalty of perjury that I prepared this application at the request of the above person. The answers provided are based on information of which I have personal knowledge and/or were provided to me by the above named person in response to the *exact questions* contained on this form.

Preparer's Printed Name

Preparer's Signature

Date *(Month/Day/Year)*

__ __ / __ __ / __ __ __ __

Preparer's Firm or Organization Name *(if applicable)*

Preparer's Daytime Phone Number

(   )

Preparer's Address - Street Number and Name

City

State

ZIP Code

Do Not Complete Parts 13 and 14 Until an INS Officer Instructs You To Do So

Part 13. Signature at Interview

I swear (affirm) and certify under penalty of perjury under the laws of the United States of America that I know that the contents of this application for naturalization subscribed by me, including corrections numbered 1 through ____ and the evidence submitted by me numbered pages 1 through ____, are true and correct to the best of my knowledge and belief.

Subscribed and sworn to before me.

Complete Signature of Applicant

Officer's Signature

Officer's Printed Name or Stamp

Date *(Month/Day/Year)*

Part 14. Oath of Allegiance

I hereby declare, on oath, that I absolutely and entirely renounce and abjure all allegiance and fidelity to any foreign prince, potentate, state, or sovereignty, of whom or which I have heretofore been a subject or citizen;
that I will support and defend the Constitution and laws of the United States of America against all enemies, foreign and domestic;
that I will bear true faith and allegiance to the same;
that I will bear arms on behalf of the United States when required by the law;
that I will perform noncombatant service in the Armed Forces of the United States when required by the law;
that I will perform work of national importance under civilian direction when required by the law; and
that I take this obligation freely, without any mental reservation or purpose of evasion; so help me God.

Printed Name of Applicant

Complete Signature of Applicant

Form N-400 (Rev. 2/11/2000)N

INS 100 Questions and Answers

Questions

1. What are the colors of our flag?
2. How many stars are there in our flag?
3. What color are the stars on our flag?
4. What do the stars on the flag mean?
5. How many stripes are there in the flag?
6. What color are the stripes?
7. What do the stripes on the flag mean?
8. How many states are there in the union?
9. What is the 4th of July?
10. What is the date of Independence Day?
11. Independence from whom?
12. What country did we fight during the Revolutionary War?
13. Who was the first president of the United States?
14. Who is the president of the United States today?
15. Who is the vice president of the United States today?
16. Who elects the president of the United States?
17. Who becomes president of the United States if the president should die?
18. For how long do we elect the president?
19. What is the Constitution?
20. Can the Constitution be changed?
21. What do we call a change to the Constitution?
22. How many changes or amendments are there to the Constitution?
23. How many branches are there in our government?
24. What are the three branches of our government?
25. What is the legislative branch of our government?
26. Who makes the laws in the United States?
27. What is Congress?
28. What are the duties of Congress?
29. Who elects Congress?
30. How many senators are there in Congress?
31. Can you name the two senators from your state?
32. For how long do we elect each senator?
33. How many representatives are there in Congress?
34. For how long do we elect the representatives?
35. What is the executive branch of our government?
36. What is the judiciary branch of our government?
37. What are the duties of the Supreme Court?
38. What is the supreme law of the United States?

39. What is the Bill of Rights?
40. What is the capital of your state?
41. Who is the current governor of your state?
42. Who becomes president of the U.S. if the president and the vice president should die?
43. Who is the chief justice of the Supreme Court?
44. Can you name the thirteen original states?
45. Who said, "Give me liberty or give me death"?
46. Which countries were our enemies during World War II?
47. What are the 49th and 50th states of the union?
48. How many terms can a president serve?
49. Who was Martin Luther King, Jr.?
50. Who is the head of your local government?
51. According to the Constitution, a person must meet certain requirements in order to be eligible to become president. Name one of these requirements.
52. Why are there 100 senators in the Senate?
53. Who selects the Supreme Court justices?
54. How many Supreme Court justices are there?
55. Why did the pilgrims come to America?
56. What is the head executive of a state government called?
57. What is the head executive of a city government called?
58. What holiday was celebrated for the first time by the American colonists?
59. Who was the main writer of the Declaration of Independence?
60. When was the Declaration of Independence adopted?
61. What is the basic belief of the Declaration of Independence?
62. What is the national anthem of the United States?
63. Who wrote the Star-Spangled Banner?
64. Where does freedom of speech come from?
65. What is the minimum voting age in the United States?
66. Who signs bills into law?
67. What is the highest court in the United States?
68. Who was the president during the Civil War?
69. What did the Emancipation Proclamation do?
70. What special group advises the president?
71. Which president is called the "father of our country"?
72. What immigration and naturalization service form is used to apply to become a naturalized citizen?
73. Who helped the pilgrims in America?

74. What is the name of the ship that brought the pilgrims to America?
75. What were the 13 original states of the United States called?
76. Name 3 rights or freedoms guaranteed by the bill of rights.
77. Who has the power to declare war?
78. What kind of government does the United States have?
79. Which president freed the slaves?
80. In what year was the Constitution written?
81. What are the first 10 amendments to the Constitution called?
82. Name one purpose of the United Nations.
83. Where does Congress meet?
84. Whose rights are guaranteed by the Constitution and the Bill of Rights?
85. What is the introduction to the Constitution called?
86. Name one benefit of being a citizen of the United States.
87. What is the most important right granted to U.S. citizens?
88. What is the United States capitol?
89. What is the White House?
90. Where is the White House located?
91. What is the name of the president's official home?
92. Name one right guaranteed by the first amendment.
93. Who is the commander in chief of the U.S. military?
94. Which president was the first commander in chief of the U.S. military?
95. In what month do we vote for the president?
96. In what month is the new president inaugurated?
97. How many times may a senator be re-elected?
98. How many times may a congressman be re-elected?
99. What are the 2 major political parties in the U.S. today?
100. How many states are there in the United States?

INS 100 Questions and Answers

Answers

1. Red, white, and blue
2. 50
3. White
4. One for each state in the union
5. 13
6. Red and white
7. They represent the original 13 states
8. 50
9. Independence Day
10. July 4th
11. England
12. England
13. George Washington
14. (insert current information)
15. (insert current information)
16. The electoral college
17. Vice president
18. Four years
19. The supreme law of the land
20. Yes
21. Amendments
22. 27
23. 3
24. Legislative, executive, and judiciary
25. Congress
26. Congress
27. The Senate and the House of Representatives
28. To make laws
29. The people
30. 100
31. (insert local information)
32. 6 years
33. 435
34. 2 years
35. The president, cabinet, and departments under the cabinet members
36. The Supreme Court
37. To interpret laws
38. The Constitution
39. The first 10 amendments of the Constitution

40. (insert local information)
41. (insert local information)
42. Speaker of the House of Representatives
43. William Rehnquist
44. Connecticut, New Hampshire, New York, New Jersey, Massachusetts, Pennsylvania, Delaware, Virginia, North Carolina, South Carolina, Georgia, Rhode Island, and Maryland
45. Patrick Henry
46. Germany, Italy, and Japan
47. Alaska and Hawaii
48. 2
49. A civil rights leader
50. (Insert local information)
51. Must be a natural born citizen of the United States; must be at least 35 years old by the time he/she will serve; must have lived in the United States for at least 14 years
52. Two (2) from each state
53. Appointed by the president
54. Nine (9)
55. For religious freedom
56. Governor
57. Mayor
58. Thanksgiving
59. Thomas Jefferson
60. July 4, 1776
61. That all men are created equal
62. The Star-Spangled Banner
63. Francis Scott Key
64. The Bill of Rights
65. Eighteen (18)
66. The president
67. The Supreme Court
68. Abraham Lincoln
69. Freed many slaves
70. The cabinet
71. George Washington
72. Form N-400, Application for Naturalization
73. The American Indians (Native Americans)
74. The Mayflower
75. Colonies
76. (a) the right of freedom of speech, press, religion, peaceable assembly and Requesting change of government. (b) the right to

bear arms (the right to have weapons or own a gun, though subject to certain regulations). (c) the government may not quarter, or house, soldiers in the people's Homes during peacetime without the people's consent. (d) the government may not search or take a person's property without a warrant. (e) a person may not be tried twice for the same crime and does not have to testify against himself. (f) a person charged with a crime still has some rights, such as the right to a trial and to have a lawyer. (g) the right to trial by jury in most cases. (h) protects people against excessive or unreasonable fines or cruel and unusual punishment. (i) the people have rights other than those mentioned in the Constitution.
(j) Any power not given to the federal government by the Constitution is a power of either the state or the people.
77. The Congress
78. Republican
79. Abraham Lincoln
80. 1787
81. The Bill of Rights
82. For countries to discuss and try to resolve world problems; to provide economic aid to many countries.
83. In the capitol in Washington, D.C.
84. Everyone (citizens and non-citizens) living in the U.S.
85. The preamble
86. Obtain federal government jobs; travel with a U.S. passport; petition for close relatives to come to the U.S. to live
87. The right to vote
88. The place where Congress meets
89. The president's official home
90. Washington, D.C. (1600 Pennsylvania Avenue, NW)
91. The White House
92. Freedom of: speech, press, religion, peaceable assembly, and requesting change of the government
93. The president
94. George Washington
95. November
96. January
97. There is no limit.
98. There is no limit.
99. Democratic and Republican
100. (50)